Individual
Rights and Civic
Responsibility

WOMEN'S RIGHTS

Jacqueline Ching and Juliet Ching

The Rosen Publishing Group, Inc.
New York

Published in 2001 by The Rosen Publishing Group, Inc.
29 East 21st Street, New York, NY 10010

Cover image: The Constitution of the United States of America

Library of Congress Cataloging-in-Publication Data

Ching, Jacqueline.
    Women's rights / by Jacqueline Ching and Juliet Ching. — 1st ed.
        p.   cm. (Individual rights and civic responsibility)
    Includes bibliographical references and index.
        ISBN 0-8239-3233-8 (lib. binding)
    1. Women's rights—United States—History. I. Ching, Juliet. II. Title. III. Series.
    HQ1236.5.U6 C49 2000
    305.42'0973—dc21

                                                                00-010354

Manufactured in the United States of America

About the Authors

Jacqueline Ching is a New York–based writer and editor. *Women's Rights* is her fifth book for the Rosen Publishing Group.

Juliet Ching is a writer and copy editor based in Portland, Oregon. She is a graduate of Georgetown University Law Center. *Women's Rights* is her first book for the Rosen Publishing Group.

For our parents, Vivien Kiang and Tan Ching

Contents

Introduction

Every year on the Fourth of July, Americans celebrate the anniversary of the Declaration of Independence. On that day, we celebrate the liberty of all the citizens of the United States of America. As we celebrate, we might ask ourselves what "liberty" means. How do we define it? How is our liberty guaranteed? How can we tell when our liberty is denied?

The Declaration of Independence, along with the United States Constitution, are remembered on that day because these documents define the concepts of national identity and citizenship in the United States of America. As citizens, we expect religious freedom, the ability to speak freely without persecution, and the right of people to have a voice in government, among other rights. Our founding fathers created a new nation under the principles of life, liberty, and the pursuit of happiness, and provided a land of opportunity for the immigrants of the seventeenth and eighteenth centuries.

As James Madison, the fourth president of the United States, wrote, "Nothing has excited more admiration than the manner in which free governments have been established in America; for it was the first instance . . . that free inhabitants have been seen deliberating on a form of government, and selecting such of their citizens as possessed their confidence to determine upon and give effect to it."

Yet consider that women did not win the right to vote until 1920, over a century after the establishment of the United States. In light of this, how are we to judge the achievements of the framers of the United States Constitution?

To answer the question of whether liberty can be given: It is never given, but rather it is won. The story of the founding of the United States of America and the writing of the Constitution show this to be true. Men of intellect and courage envisioned a government that was a balance between authority and liberty, and they struggled to achieve it—but they did not include women. The story of the women's rights movement proves that achieving freedom for all is a struggle that continues.

Colonial America

When the Declaration of Independence was written and signed on July 4, 1776, there was no United States of America. Americans were neither united nor autonomous. Instead, there existed thirteen colonies, settled by Great Britain and located along the Atlantic coast of North America. (Spain and France had colonized other parts of North America.) These thirteen colonies were New

Hampshire, Massachusetts, Rhode Island, Connecticut, New York, New Jersey, Pennsylvania, Delaware, Maryland, Virginia, North Carolina, South Carolina, and Georgia.

The Declaration of Independence stated the basic principles of constitutional government but did not establish that government. Americans would have to wait until more than a dozen years later, after the Revolutionary War with Great Britain had been fought, for the constitution that made the thirteen colonies into one nation to be adopted. The thirteen colonies struggled and eventually won independence from Great Britain. Initially, however, they were without an adequate constitution or any system of law.

The states remained sovereign—meaning that they were functional as separate countries, lacking the power to act together. In the absence of a strong national government, the states disagreed on issues of interest to all, such as tax collection, trade policies, national defense, and civil rights. Marked distinctions existed between the states, especially between the industrialized New England states and the agrarian (farming) states of the South. This meant that what was in the best interest of the North, for instance, might not be in the best interest of the South. These were the problems that faced the framers of the United States Constitution.

Less than a quarter of a century earlier, however, most Americans would have found it difficult to imagine that they might one day need a separate constitution. While part of the British Empire, the colonies benefited from their mother country's system of international trade and military protection. As long as the colonies were left alone to manage their own affairs, it was easy enough, for a time, to overlook the basic differences between the colonies and Great Britain.

How did these differences develop? The unique identity of the new land—what would eventually be called America—grew from the experiences of the people who colonized it. The Europeans who landed there hoped for better economic opportunities. But more than anything else, they were fleeing the religious upheavals and political oppression of the sixteenth and seventeenth centuries. Among them were intellectuals, learned individuals who believed in representative government. It troubled them that the colonies were bound to follow English law and to pay taxes to Great Britain, yet had no representation in the English Parliament.

The freedom of the new land, helped by its distance from its mother country, enabled thinkers like Thomas Jefferson and Benjamin Franklin to explore the ethics and philosophies that came to dominate the American intellectual landscape. In addition, the blending of cultures—Dutch, English, Scottish, Irish, French, and German, among others—contributed to the growing political and cultural rift between Great Britain and the colonies. As long as Great Britain left the colonies alone, they could mostly ignore these differences. But once Great Britain began to exert its power, the colonies were forced to fight for their freedom.

In the 1760s, following the French and Indian War, Great Britain found itself burdened with vast debts. It decided that a solution to this problem could be found in increasing revenue from the colonies. It could collect this revenue by increasing the taxes on goods bought and sold in the colonies.

In 1764, Parliament passed the Sugar Act, the first law aimed specifically at raising tax revenue from the colonies. Then came the Currency Act, which prohibited the colonies from issuing their own money, or currency. These were followed by other laws much hated by the colonists, such as the Stamp Act, designed to pay for the British troops stationed in the colonies. The passage of these acts triggered organized—as well as violent—resistance. They angered the people of the colonies and changed public opinion.

Many colonists who once valued their membership in the British Empire came to believe that the colonies needed to unite to win freedom. In 1775, clashes between colonial patriots and British soldiers led to the War of Independence, or the American Revolution. The following year, the colonies declared their independence from Great Britain by signing the Declaration of Independence.

Toward a Stronger Union

The American Revolution continued until the British surrendered in 1781. But it was not until 1783 that Great Britain finally recognized the independence of the thirteen American states. The Articles of Confederation, drafted in 1781, were meant to unite what were still essentially thirteen separate countries. But mindful of their experience under British central authority, the drafters of the articles actually established a confederation of sovereign states. Even with the Articles of Confederation, the American government was weak and ineffective and lacked the powers to tax or even to enforce laws within the states.

Finally, in the summer of 1787, a group of fifty-five delegates met in Philadelphia with the intent of amending the Articles of Confederation. Instead, they ended up writing a whole new document—what would become the United States Constitution. The framers of the Constitution embodied the attitude of the new nation—an awareness of the lessons handed down from their European ancestors combined with a brave new optimism for the future.

The experiences that led up to the American Revolution made the drafters of the Constitution particularly concerned with limiting the power of the government while protecting the liberty of individuals. They believed in the concept of balance—a separation of powers in politics, as outlined by the French philosopher Baron de Montesquieu in *The Spirit of the Laws*. They established the three separate branches of government that remain to this day: the executive (the president), the legislative (Congress), and the judicial (the Supreme Court). Each branch ensures that the others do not gain too much power; this is known as a system of checks and balances.

The Constitution gave Congress substantial power over the young country's economic and financial affairs. Congress would collect taxes, issue money, borrow on the national credit, grant patents and copyrights, establish post offices and roads, regulate interstate commerce, and establish and maintain the military. It could also declare war. Congress would also be responsible for managing international relations and passing related laws, such as those that would allow foreigners to become citizens.

On September 17, 1787, thirty-nine delegates signed the completed draft of the Constitution. It was now ready to be tried in the court of public opinion. Nine of the thirteen states had to accept it in order for it to be ratified, or approved. If a ninth state ratified the Constitution, Congress

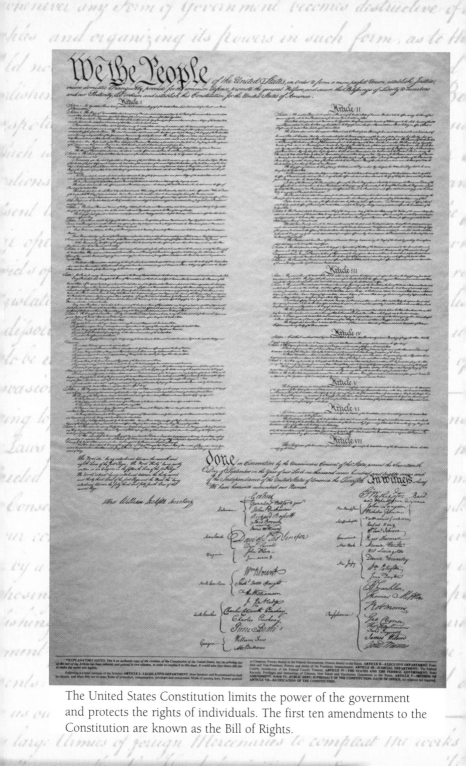

The United States Constitution limits the power of the government and protects the rights of individuals. The first ten amendments to the Constitution are known as the Bill of Rights.

would set March 4, 1789, as the date for the new government to begin its proceedings.

The Bill of Rights

In many states, the ratification of the Constitution hinged on the promised addition of twelve amendments, or improvements, to the document's seven original articles. Ten of the amendments were ratified in 1791. These ten amendments became known as the Bill of Rights.

The guarantees put forth in the Bill of Rights are legally binding. This means that if, for example, an act of Congress (the legislative branch) is found to violate the principles of the Constitution, the act may be voided by the United States Supreme Court (the judicial branch). This is one way in which the system of checks and balances works.

The Amendments

The First Amendment of the Bill of Rights protects five of the most basic American liberties: freedom of religion, freedom of speech, freedom of the press, freedom of assembly, and freedom to petition the government.

The Second and Third Amendments were created specifically to address certain experiences the colonists had while under British rule. As British citizens, they were not allowed to keep or bear arms. The government feared that the citizens might use these weapons in an insurrection. But the Second Amendment provided that the American people have the right to "keep and bear arms." The Third Amendment provided that, in peacetime, citizens would not be made to keep soldiers in their homes without consent.

This was because colonists had been forced to house and feed British soldiers during the Revolutionary War.

Today, some Americans firmly believe that the Second Amendment is a right that should still be extended to law-abiding citizens of the United States. Others believe that, much like the Third Amendment, it is an artifact of colonial times. These people usually advocate gun control.

The Fourth Amendment protects citizens from "unreasonable searches and seizures" of their bodies, possessions, or homes. The Fifth Amendment is quite well known. In crime movies and novels, the accused character will often "take the Fifth." The Fifth Amendment guarantees the accused protection against self-incrimination. It is also informally known as "the right to remain silent." Thus, people cannot be forced, by torture or other means, to confess to crimes they may or may not have committed. The Fifth Amendment also guarantees the accused due process of the law and assumes that he or she is innocent until proven guilty.

The Sixth Amendment guarantees the right to a speedy trial, an impartial jury, and the right of the accused to confront his or her accuser(s). The Seventh Amendment guarantees the right of trial by jury and the Eighth protects the convicted from cruel and unusual punishment.

The Ninth Amendment states that the Constitution and the Bill of Rights do not define all the fundamental rights of citizens. It also asserts that such rights exist whether or not they are defined. The Tenth Amendment makes a similar claim concerning the rights of states and citizens—that the people grant power to the government.

A Timeless Document

Because the Constitution is the basis of American government, it is as crucial today as it was when the nation was founded. It organizes the country's basic political institutions. It guarantees individual rights. But perhaps the most important aspect of the U.S. Constitution is that it is sufficiently elastic to meet the needs of later generations and of a greatly expanded body politic.

Foreseeing the future need to possibly change or add to the document, the framers of the Constitution included an article that would allow for its amendment. The Constitution cannot be changed in any way, except by the process of amendment outlined in Article V, which requires a two-thirds vote of both houses of Congress. (States also have the power to propose amendments, but this method has never been used.) Twenty-seven amendments have been added to the Constitution since it was drafted in 1789. The Nineteenth Amendment, passed in 1920, granted women the right to vote.

1 The First Steps

Imagine that because you are a woman, your opinion does not count. Imagine that you—as well as your mother, sisters, friends, and aunts—are not allowed to speak out in public. Imagine not even having the same rights under constitutional law that men take for granted.

This was how things were not that long ago in the United States of America—where the founding fathers wrote one of the greatest treatises on democracy, the Constitution of the United States. Today, the United States is generally thought of as synonymous with individual freedom, equality, and expression. Yet how could it be that less than a hundred years ago, half the adult population could not vote simply because they were women?

In the early days of the republic, only men of property enjoyed full rights of citizenship, while the rest of the population had to fight for rights as basic as being able to speak out in public. The fight for women's rights continues to this day, as women struggle to have the same rights as men in areas such as employment—being paid the same amount of money for the same kind of work and being offered the same opportunities for promotion.

The First Immigrants

The first settlers who came to the colonies had to bring with them everything they would need in their new lives. This included the legal system that they had used in England. Before the colonies created their own set of laws, they continued to operate under English Common Law.

Under English Common Law, an unmarried woman had all the rights of a man, except for suffrage, or the right to vote. She could sue and be sued, keep the wages that she earned, enter into legal contracts, own or sell property, and freely choose her legal heirs. On the other hand, once a woman was married, she lost her legal identity. In the eyes of the law, a married woman was merely a part of her husband's identity. Not only did she lose the legal rights she had as a single woman, but a married woman's body belonged legally to her husband as well. She had no say in whether or not she wanted children, or how many she wanted to have. If her husband beat her, it was within his legal rights to do so. If another person injured a married woman, it was the woman's husband who could claim the legal right to sue for damages and compensation. In other words, upon marriage, a woman effectively became a child in the eyes of the law.

The status of women in the thirteen colonies was the result of a patriarchal society, in which women derived their status solely from that of the men to whom they were married or related. Not all societies at the time were patriarchal,

17

however. In contrast to the English system, Native American communities were often matriarchal societies, where the power rested in the hands of the female elders of the tribe.

However, poor women in Europe had few economic opportunities, and no educational ones. The legal identity they had as single women did not mean much. In order to obtain the basic necessities, their only real option was to marry, even though becoming a wife lowered a woman's legal status. Furthermore, there was a social stigma attached to being an unmarried woman. There were only a few years in a young woman's life in which she was considered eligible for marriage. After these prime years passed, it became harder and harder for a woman to find a husband. Lacking a husband or economic opportunities, a woman's livelihood might be at risk as she aged. Under these conditions, it is not difficult to understand why poor women risked their lives to travel to an unknown new world.

In the earliest days, the colonies—populated with soldiers, farmers, and travelers—were desperate for women. They often bribed European women to make the hazardous journey across the sea. These women were willing to immigrate to the colonies because they were desperate to improve their economic conditions—even at the cost of their personal freedom. Sometimes they paid for the cost of their ocean passage by becoming indentured servants, often for as long as seven years. As indentured servants, these women had to work for free for the specified number of years, and could not marry without the consent of their "masters."

Women also came over from Europe as "tobacco brides" to be auctioned off to tobacco farmers in the South. With the rise of the slave trade in the seventeenth and eighteenth centuries, African women, as well as men, were kidnapped from their homes and shipped to the colonies. In circumstances where there were no European women, the colonists cohabited with the Native American women.

Because of the harsh conditions in the colonies, and the fact that colonists were often ill prepared for their new life, colonial men and women had to endure hardships together. They had to share labor equally. This blurred the boundaries between men and women somewhat, and gave women opportunities and a certain amount of autonomy that they did not have before. This was especially true in the southern colonies where tobacco was planted because women were required to work in the fields alongside the men. The rougher the conditions of work, the less strictly old social customs were followed. This gave southern women some flexibility and improvements in social status, which women in the North did not have. For example, in New England's Puritan colonies, where the economy was not based on farming, social conditions were strictly patterned after England. Therefore, women's social status did not improve as readily.

Early Activism and the Revolutionary War

Life in the colonies offered many new opportunities. At the same time, it also gave women a new vision of themselves and of their world. Injustices were no longer necessarily accepted. One of the first national women's organizations, the Daughters of Liberty, was formed as a result of an economic boycott in 1769 to protest English taxes on goods imported to the colonies. The Daughters of Liberty supported the boycott to help eliminate the colonies' reliance on English imports. Within a year of the boycott, the English repealed the taxes. This was the first demonstration of the effectiveness of an organized effort by women.

Before the birth of the republic, colonial men were, in some ways, no better off than colonial women. As colonists, men were not allowed very much political participation. Most of the important issues, such as taxation, were still decided by the English. Voting was limited to the relatively small number of property owners. Suffrage, or the right to vote, was not an issue on many people's minds. But, like the women, men in the colonies also began to see new possibilities. This eventually led to the belief that England should no longer rule over the colonies, and the Revolutionary War began. When women began to recognize the injustice of their situation, they, too, would wage a war of their own, albeit a much different kind of war that would last a much longer time.

Throughout the history of the women's movement, wars provided the greatest impetus for change. The harsh living and working conditions of the colonial South had made the women there more equal to men out of necessity—at least in practice, if not legislatively. Similar opportunities were provided by periods of war. When the American Revolution broke out in the middle of the eighteenth century, it provided a chance for women to show that they could be equal to men. While men were called to the battlefield, women took over the management of their households and their husbands' businesses. The war gave them a chance to show that they could handle jobs traditionally done by men.

The Revolutionary War also marked the beginning of women organizing themselves into groups to achieve a common goal. They formed fund-raising groups to collect money for George Washington's army. They started spinning societies to make cloth for soldiers' uniforms. With a shortage of almost everything—food, clothing, and medicine—women's groups made significant contributions to the colonial armies. Women produced as much as they could to meet soldiers' needs.

Women had hoped that their patriotic efforts during the American Revolution would help to improve their social and economic standing in the new republic. Unfortunately, when the war ended, they received less than they had hoped. The Constitution of the newly formed republic guaranteed its citizens their rights, but the Constitution did not specifically mention women. By omitting women from the document, the Constitution left open matters of law relating to women. As a result, women were excluded from political participation in the new republic. They were not full citizens.

In fact, the Constitution was written only to provide rights to the white male property owners of the population. Women, who had contributed in many significant ways during the Revolutionary War against England, gained no political or economic advantage as a result of their efforts. The men of the colonies fought a bitter war for their rights, but in the end kept those rights to themselves just as the English had done.

Early Days of the Suffrage Movement

The language of the Constitution did not explicitly deny women the right to vote. But in effect, nothing in the colonies had changed after the Revolutionary War, except in one state—New Jersey. The elected officials of New Jersey were largely from the Quaker community, which had always supported the role of women as leaders. A New Jersey statute was passed in 1783 to grant voting rights to "all inhabitants of this state, of full age, who are worth fifty pounds proclamation money." Thus, New Jersey became the first and only state to grant suffrage to women in the new nation.

This early foray into women's suffrage was short-lived, however. At first, very few women in New Jersey voted. Then, as more and more women began to cast their votes in local elections, the power of the women's vote became apparent. There were almost enough votes from women to alter the outcome of a heated election in 1797. The candidate that the women supported nearly won; his opponent beat him by a very small margin. This was a wake-up call to those who had underestimated the power of the woman voter. For the first time, men had to take the opinions of women seriously—and this frightened many of them. Critics of the women's suffrage movement became more vocal and aggressive. The idea that women could determine the outcome of an election was too much for them to bear. What if the women elected their own candidates to office? This possibility was not something the antisuffragists were ready to accept. Many men did not mind women having the vote—so long as the women did not exercise that right!

The critics of women's suffrage made repeated attempts to repeal the statute in the New Jersey legislature. But again and again, it was upheld. Finally, the matter came to a head. In 1806, a poorly organized election created an atmosphere of chaos, where charges of fraud were ultimately made against the voters. Both men and women were accused of voting more than once, and charges of illegal voting were made against slaves who had allegedly been admitted illegally into polling stations. But instead of a full investigation into the charges, women were quickly turned into scapegoats. Women were blamed for creating the chaotic atmosphere. A new statute was passed in 1807 prohibiting women and other "undesirables" from voting.

Early Advocates of Women's Rights

One of the early advocates of women's rights was Abigail Adams. In a famous letter to John Adams, her husband and the second president of the United States, she begged him to "Remember the Ladies, and be more generous and favorable to them than your ancestors. Do not put such unlimited power into the hands of the Husbands." Her husband rebuffed this request. "Depend upon it, we know better than to repeal our Masculine systems," he responded. It was a sentiment that was popular at the time. Historians continue to debate whether Abigail Adams sought to make women more equal to men only within the domestic sphere or in the public sphere as well. But one thing about her was certain: She was one of the earliest advocates of equal educational opportunities for all, regardless of sex or race.

The fight for women's rights was indeed an uphill battle. Without access to a good education, there was little chance for a woman to attain anything near full equality with a man. Even if women had the vote, without greater independence and a better education, they were little more than pawns in the game of politics. In fact, this was the argument John Adams used against the idea of women's suffrage. If a married woman had no separate legal identity but was merely a legal extension of her husband, and given the limited scope of her political experience, then wouldn't her husband just tell her how to vote? It was as if married men would be voting twice! But without the vote, women could not have any influence on the laws that were passed. They would always remain second-class citizens and be subjected to the wishes of men. As a result, the laws that were passed were often unfair to women. For example, prostitution was a crime for which only women were punished. Women were caught in a vicious circle. The right and opportunity to have an education would be a primary concern in the fight for equality.

Another early advocate of women's rights was an Englishwoman named Mary Wollstonecraft. She was inspired by the political events taking place in France, where reformers fought for equality for all men, a period in French history that was to evolve into the French Revolution. She wrote a book called *A Vindication of the Rights of Women*, which was published in America in 1792. In it, she challenged the common notion that women were inferior, both in mind and body, to men. She countered that if women had the same access to education as men did, then there would be no reason for women to be intellectually inferior to men. She also stressed the importance of physical education to maintain a strong, healthy body. During the second half of the nineteenth century, Wollstonecraft's book was dismissed as too radical by some leading feminist thinkers of the day. It was not until the very end of the century that Susan B. Anthony and Elizabeth Cady Stanton, two of the most prominent suffragist leaders, recognized Wollstonecraft's contribution to the women's liberation cause.

One of Wollstonecraft's contemporaries, Judith Sargent Stevens Murray, also attributed the difference between men and women to the discriminatory practices in education for boys and girls. "How is the one exalted and the other depressed . . . The one is taught to aspire, and the other is early confined and limited," Murray wrote. Two hundred years later, this remains a critical issue in education. Are boys encouraged to pursue mathematics and sciences while girls are encouraged to pursue the arts? Gender bias is still in effect today, and this remains true in the field of education. For example, the teaching profession, because it is a traditionally acceptable career for women, commands less respect and less pay than other professions like law or medicine. This was true in the nineteenth century and is still true today.

In September 1821, the first high school solely for girls was established in Troy, New York. The Troy Female Seminary was established by America's leading woman educator of the time, Emma Willard. She lobbied tirelessly for state funding for the higher education of women—first in Connecticut, then in New York. She landed in Troy because the city offered her $4,000 to set up the school. The Troy Female Seminary trained women to believe in their own abilities and to trust their own judgments rather than defer to men.

Other schools were soon established that offered women higher education comparable to that found in men's schools. The curricula of the new schools consisted of subjects never before taught to women—physics, chemistry, mathematics, geography, and history. Mount Holyoke College in central Massachusetts, the oldest women's college in America, was established in 1837. Oberlin College, founded in 1833, was the first institution to offer a coeducational program that was open not only to whites but blacks as well. In 1846, Oberlin held the first public debate on women's suffrage.

Reform Movements in the Early Nineteenth Century

With the opening of women's schools, the first half of the nineteenth century provided women with greater educational opportunities than ever before. It was also a time of other great changes for women. Women, who had been forbidden to do any kind of public speaking, began to speak out publicly as they became activists in different social reform movements. The first woman to speak out publicly was Fanny Wright, a Scottish heiress who renounced the life of leisure and immigrated to America to become a public lecturer, speaking out against the social ills of the day. Other women like her, in great numbers, organized reform groups to promote temperance, labor reform, abolition, and equal rights. These social reform movements provided women with an invaluable opportunity to participate in political and public life. Their experience in these movements would shape their future efforts in the suffrage movement.

The North was industrializing rapidly, and large numbers of factories sprang up, mostly in the booming textile industry. As many women began to work in factories, they learned how to strike in order to protest unfair labor practices. In 1834, when the owners of Lowell Mills in Lowell, Massachusetts, threatened to implement a 15 percent wage cutback, the women went on strike. Although that strike and several others that followed did not achieve the goals of more equitable wages and shorter working hours, the women at Lowell learned valuable lessons in organization. In 1844, the women formed the Lowell Female Labor Reform Association, headed by Sarah Bagley. They obtained thousands of signatures on their petitions and used the local labor newspaper to spread their agenda. Eventually, in 1874, they achieved a ten-hour workday. The mill owners never again underestimated the collective power of their women employees.

The effect of these social movements on the women's suffrage movement, while mostly indirect, was nonetheless significant. It gave women a taste of the political life. Women learned how to organize large groups of people, how to speak out publicly and effectively, and how to use political methods. They brought their causes from door to door, handing out pamphlets and getting signatures on petitions. Later on, under the leadership of Emmeline Pankhurst, a leading British suffragist who favored militant methods, women activists employed even more aggressive tactics, such as holding parades, wearing sandwich boards, and participating in outdoor demonstrations.

The Antislavery Movement

Before there was an official women's rights movement, women activists involved themselves in the antislavery movement. In 1833, Lucretia Mott, who was to become a leading figure in the women's suffrage movement, helped form the Philadelphia Female Anti-Slavery Society. Within the next four years, there were over a thousand antislavery groups, including the Female Anti-Slavery Society, formed by a group of African American women. Membership in these groups was divided equally between men and women, and in total the groups had about 150,000 members.

The Seneca Falls Convention

One result of women's participation in the abolitionist movement was that many of the leaders in that movement later became the most prominent and outspoken champions of women's suffrage. Indeed, many of them became acquainted with each other at antislavery conventions. The convention at Seneca Falls is often considered the official beginning of the women's rights movement. It came about because Lucretia Mott had traveled to London in order to attend the World Anti-Slavery Conference in 1840 but was denied admission because she was a woman. There, she met Elizabeth Cady Stanton, who was also not allowed to

The Seneca Falls convention of 1848 is often considered the official beginning of the women's rights movement. This political cartoon satirized the convention.

participate in the convention. Ironically, as we will discuss later, developments in the antislavery movement in the United States caused abolitionists and feminists to separate the two movements, for the most part.

After Mott and Stanton were refused admission to the World Anti-Slavery Conference, they decided that it was time women held a conference of their own. The Seneca Falls convention was held in 1848. The convention featured a Declaration of Sentiments, modeled after the Declaration of Independence. It opened with the words, "We hold these truths to be self-evident: That all men and women are created equal." The conventioneers adopted twelve resolutions concerning the rights of women—not special rights, but rights that men already enjoyed. It can be difficult to fathom a time when women had to fight for the right to own property, to keep the wages that they earned, or to have custody of their children in cases of divorce. But it was once considered very radical for women to seek equal rights.

The Civil War

From 1861 to 1865, the states of the North and South fought the Civil War over the issue of slavery. Once again, women had opportunities to do things they could not do during peacetime. As men went off to war, women took care of the labor shortages on the home front. They did whatever needed to be done. Informal ladies' societies and more formally organized groups such as the Sanitary Commission raised money and collected supplies for the armies. But while nurses took care of the wounded on the battlefield and in the hospitals, women doctors were discouraged from joining the army. In some instances, wives of army officers accompanied their husbands to the battlefield. Perhaps most remarkable, however, is that as many as four hundred women served in the war as soldiers while disguised as men.

Like the Revolutionary War, the Civil War gave women a chance to do something other than cook, clean, and take care of their families. But after the war was over, their contributions to the war were again overlooked. Women's labor was given no value, whether it was in the home or on the battlefield. After the Civil War, the political status of white women had changed little. But the end of slavery meant that African American women in the South, along with African American men, were now free. Yet, like their white counterparts, there was still a long way for African American women to go to achieve equality with men. Educational and economic opportunities remained limited for African American women in the South. Those who could, moved to the North, where there were greater opportunities for work and learning.

African American Suffragists

If you were an African American woman in the nineteenth century, not only did you have to fight for women's justice, but for your very freedom as well. Historically, the fight against slavery was an integral part of the fight for women's rights. Sojourner Truth, a former slave who ran away and became a public speaker, was a crusader against slavery and also a champion of women's rights. Truth was unlike other early African American women activists because most of the others were born free and were often educated. Some even came from privileged backgrounds. Truth, on the other hand, was illiterate. She continued doing menial work even after she was freed. But she possessed the gift of rhetoric and spoke with so much passion that her speeches often attracted large crowds. She spoke eloquently about the plight of the black woman: "There is a great stir about colored men getting their rights, and not colored women theirs; you see the colored men will be masters over the women, and it will be just as bad as it was before."

In the time before the Civil War, called the antebellum period, it was uncommon for the ideas and speeches of African American abolitionist movement leaders to be recorded; Sojourner Truth was the exception. Among the abolitionist leaders who were not recorded were Harriet

31

Forten Purvis and her sister Margaretta Forten, who helped found the Philadelphia Female Anti-Slavery Society; Charlotte (Lottie) Rollin, the first South Carolina delegate to a women's suffrage convention; and militant abolitionist Mary Ann Cary. These women left no written records of their thoughts and ideas, even though they gave many speeches throughout their careers. These activists were involved in organizations that sought to improve the socio-economic status and political power of all women, but the political arguments of these African American women activists were not regularly recorded until the 1870s.

By the end of the nineteenth century, more and more African American women had mobilized to join or form organizations in support of women's suffrage. Because of the reluctance of some white suffragists to include African American women in their organizations, many African American women formed their own organizations. As a result, many important African American leaders emerged during this period.

In 1896, the National Association of Colored Women (NACW) was formed when two of its forerunners—the National Federation of Afro-American Women and the National League of Colored Women—joined together. Its founders were Frances Harper and Mary Church Terrell. Mary Church Terrell, born in Tennessee to slave parents, was its first president. She graduated from Oberlin College in 1884 and was fluent not only in English but also in French and German. Terrell was the first African American woman to be on the board of education in the District of Columbia. She helped to establish the Women Wage Earners' Association because African American women were

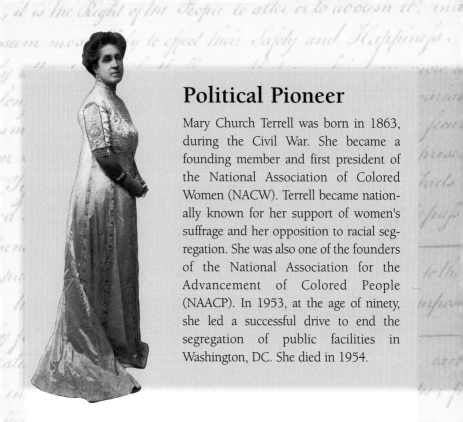

Political Pioneer

Mary Church Terrell was born in 1863, during the Civil War. She became a founding member and first president of the National Association of Colored Women (NACW). Terrell became nationally known for her support of women's suffrage and her opposition to racial segregation. She was also one of the founders of the National Association for the Advancement of Colored People (NAACP). In 1953, at the age of ninety, she led a successful drive to end the segregation of public facilities in Washington, DC. She died in 1954.

largely shut out of women's organizations and trade unions. Terrell was a speaker of international renown.

For Terrell, the fight was always twofold—gender equality between the genders went hand in hand with equality among the races. Under Terrell's leadership, the NACW forged ties with other national women's groups, such as the all-white National American Women's Suffrage Association. But in general, African American women were excluded from the all-white national women's organizations, especially in the South. Some white suffragists thought that allying with the issue of abolitionism would alienate white male voters who might otherwise be sympathetic toward women's suffrage. Later, as African American men won the right to vote before women did, tension between white suffragists and African American suffragists grew. Terrell's response to the criticisms of white suffragists was, "My sisters of the dominant race, stand up not only for the oppressed sex, but also for the oppressed race!" Nonetheless, the suffrage of African American men before suffrage of women became a divisive issue among political leaders.

Race and Gender Split

After the Civil War ended in 1865, the Fourteenth and Fifteenth Amendments were passed, recognizing African American men as full citizens and legally granting them the right to vote. But the amendments had the opposite effect on women's rights. The Fourteenth Amendment actually subverted women's rights by inserting the word "male" in the Constitution for the first time. It made it clear that only male citizens counted when determining the number of representatives for each state. It removed women yet one more step from full participation in the political process. The Fifteenth Amendment was also disappointing for the women's movement, for while it gave African American men the right to vote, it, too, left women out altogether.

The last decade of the nineteenth century and the first one of the twentieth were periods of heightened tension in American race relations. The southern states contravened, or acted against, the Fourteenth and Fifteenth Amendments by passing state legislation to exclude African Americans from voting. In addition, "Jim Crow laws" were passed, imposing racial segregation in all areas of society.

African American women had issues of both race and gender to confront. But white suffragists faced the dilemma of whether or not to associate their movement with that of African Americans. Different factions of the suffragist movement took different views as to what was the best strategy. Some hoped to persuade the southern governments that giving white women the vote was a way of excluding African Americans. Others thought that the issue of race relations was too controversial and would have a detrimental effect on the women's movement by alienating potential southern supporters.

There were activists who fought for suffrage for all men, but not women; there were those who wanted suffrage for all women, but not necessarily African American women. Most suffragist organizations, in fact, excluded African American women from membership. This did not deter African American women from having active roles in the suffragist movement. But even after suffrage was granted to women in 1920, African American women still had to fight because of southern resistance to universal suffrage. It was not until as late as 1965, as a result of the revitalized civil rights movement, that universal suffrage was finally adopted.

2 Women's Suffrage Organizations

In 1866, the American Equal Rights Association (AERA) was founded to seek suffrage for all citizens regardless of race or gender. Susan B. Anthony and Elizabeth Cady Stanton founded the organization to procure suffrage for all. For a change, not only were African American women accepted into membership, but they were also elected to key positions in the organization. Hattie Purvis, Harriet Purvis's daughter, and Frances Harper both served on the AERA's finance committee. Unfortunately, the AERA soon found itself facing a split over the issue of African American suffrage versus women's suffrage.

The AERA became even more fragmented when Anthony and Stanton began to associate themselves with George Francis Train, a millionaire from the North who was sympathetic to the southern cause. Ignoring Train's flagrant and outspoken racism, Anthony and Stanton accepted his offer of money to start a newspaper that would serve both the interests of the women's suffrage movement and Train's political ambitions. The paper was called *The Revolution* and its motto was: "Men, their rights, and nothing more; Women, their rights, and nothing less." Unfortunately, it was considered too radical for most women and folded after two years.

The AERA supported the Fifteenth Amendment and believed that giving African American men the right to vote was one step in the right direction. This stance, however, caused a major rift among the leaders of the women's rights movement. Some suffragists were outraged that African American men would get the vote before educated white women.

Anthony and Stanton were two members of the AERA who embarked on an anti-Fifteenth Amendment campaign. Lucy Stone, a suffragist leader who believed that the issues of women's rights and antislavery were intertwined and who was repulsed by Train's influence, urged them to take a more conservative approach. She argued, "I thank God for the Fifteenth Amendment, and hope that it will be adopted in every state. I will be thankful in my soul if anybody can get out of the terrible pit." Stanton published her response in an issue of *The Revolution*, stating that she did not believe "in allowing ignorant Negroes and foreigners to make laws for her to obey." Although Stanton and Anthony began their activism in the American Anti-Slavery Society in 1857 and devoted their careers to fighting both slavery and discrimination based on race or sex, they were not above using racist rhetoric to win support for women's suffrage. Finally, frustrated by the inclusion of African American men but not women in the new amendments,

The National Women's Suffrage Association, led by Susan B. Anthony (left) and Elizabeth Cady Stanton (right), drafted the Woman's Declaration of Rights in 1876.

Anthony and Stanton separated themselves completely from the abolitionists.

Different Strategies

Because of the rift, Stanton and Anthony withdrew from the AERA and formed the National Women's Suffrage Association (NWSA) in 1869. Later that same year, Lucy Stone formed the American Women's Suffrage Association (AWSA). Both organizations accepted African American members, but more African American women joined the AWSA than the NWSA.

The NWSA and the AWSA supported different strategies for winning the vote. The NWSA, led by Stanton and Anthony, believed that the only way to achieve women's suffrage was through a federal amendment to the Constitution. In 1876, the NWSA held a meeting and drafted the Woman's Declaration of Rights, which used the language of the Declaration of Independence to argue for equal rights for women. That year, a celebration was held in Philadelphia to mark the passing of one hundred years since the birth of the nation. Anthony and Stanton wanted to present this declaration as a companion piece to the Declaration of Independence at the celebration, but they were denied permission to do so.

The AWSA, on the other hand, believed that a decentralized approach might be more effective in achieving the ultimate goal of suffrage for all women. While she supported a federal amendment, Stone believed that winning suffrage one state at a time was another viable approach. She also believed in "partial suffrage," where women would be allowed to vote in local elections on certain issues, such as education. Still others, like activists Mary Ann Cary and Victoria Woodhull, felt that the Fourteenth and Fifteenth Amendments were generally steps in the right direction. They believed Congress needed to pass a more liberal interpretation of the amendments in order to allow women to vote.

Victoria Woodhull is one of the most colorful figures in the history of the women's movement. She was a free spirit, unafraid of challenges and criticisms. She led a flamboyant life that was unprecedented in the nineteenth century and might even be considered scandalous today. Her career was more like that of a vaudeville performer than of an activist—she worked as a prostitute and a psychic, then moved on to unlikely careers as a stockbroker and journalist. She also has the distinction of being the first woman to run for president of the United States.

At first, Susan B. Anthony was impressed by Woodhull's outspokenness. Woodhull argued before Congress that women be allowed to vote on the grounds that the Fourteenth and Fifteenth Amendments protected the rights of all citizens, which by definition should include women. But Woodhull also had a reputation for being an advocate of free love. Some NWSA members were afraid that Woodhull's participation would give the suffrage movement an unfavorable association. Furthermore, Woodhull was not beneath using blackmail—by threatening to publish scandalous but often false accusations in her weekly. After only one year, the NWSA wanted to have nothing more to do with her. Her alliance with the suffrage movement turned out to be a mixed blessing at best, but Woodhull pushed the envelope for the kinds of things women were "allowed" to do. She cleared a path for others to follow.

In the election year of 1872, the NWSA urged women all over the country to try to vote. These attempts did not meet with success. For example, although Mary Ann Cary successfully registered to vote in the District of Columbia, she was not allowed to actually vote. Susan B. Anthony, with a group of about fifty women, attempted to register in Rochester, New York. The election inspectors let them register only after Anthony threatened to sue them on criminal charges. Then on November 5, 1872, Anthony—this time accompanied by only fourteen women—came to the polls to cast her vote. She succeeded, but three weeks later, Anthony, the fourteen women, and the voting inspectors who had registered them were all arrested for illegal voting activity. Everyone paid a five-hundred-dollar bail—except for Anthony.

Anthony had a plan. She wanted the issue of women's suffrage to be heard by the Supreme Court of the United States. She decided that the fastest way to achieve this was to get herself arrested and jailed. Once arrested, she would refuse bail and instead petition a writ of habeas corpus. Habeas corpus is a legal petition whereby a person who is jailed can ask for immediate release unless the agency detaining him or her can meet the burden of proof of guilt for the arrest. By refusing bail and applying for habeas corpus, Anthony would either have to be released promptly or the matter would have to be determined by a court of law. If a lower court refused Anthony's petition, she could then appeal to higher and higher courts, until the matter reached the Supreme Court. There, Anthony hoped to challenge the constitutionality of the Fifteenth Amendment.

Unfortunately, Anthony's lawyer, Henry Selden, paid Anthony's bail. While he did it out of concern and respect for her, Anthony was angry at her lawyer—and disappointed that she lost her chance to confront the Supreme Court. Anthony was undeterred and decided to try again. In a second attempt to be put in jail, she voted in a local election. This time, however, the judge—fearing a sympathetic jury—directed the jury to find Anthony guilty before the hearing even began! To make matters worse, the judge saw through Anthony's tactics and refused to put her in jail until she paid her fine.

The Fifteenth Amendment was finally brought before the Supreme Court in the case of *Minor v. Happersett*. Virginia Minor was an officer of the NWSA while Reese Happersett was a voter registrar in St. Louis, Missouri. Unlike the other women who tried to vote, Minor sued Happersett for $10,000 when he refused to let her register. This time, the case did go to the Supreme Court. In 1875, the Supreme Court concluded that "the Constitution of the United States does not confer the right of suffrage upon anyone." The question of suffrage was left to each state to decide. This effectively ended any hopes of obtaining a judicial precedent for women's suffrage. The women's groups now directed their efforts toward the states and toward a federal amendment to the Constitution.

3 New Leadership, New Directions

In the closing decades of the nineteenth century, suffrage became the central issue of the women's movement. Thwarted in their efforts to appeal to the Supreme Court, women's rights activists needed to develop new strategies. It became clear that without the power to elect lawmakers who would advocate women's rights, women—even when they achieved certain reforms—would be merely winning small battles, but not the war. Women would always be inferior to men if they could not also decide what laws were passed. Their lives and rights would remain dependent on the judgments of men. Women's organizations decided to focus their efforts on obtaining suffrage. But as the groups became divided in their strategies, the movement lost some of its overall momentum and vision. Race continued to be a factor, as some white women pitted their interests against those of African American women and men. It would not be until the arrival of a new generation of leadership that the suffrage movement would regain its power.

A New Generation of Suffrage Leaders

Toward the end of the century, the differing opinions and strategies of suffragist leaders began to take a toll on the women's rights movement. The movement began to lose its general focus and direction as its leaders became older and its members became increasingly frustrated with each defeat. Finally, a new generation of suffragist leaders emerged to infuse the movement with new blood. In 1890, under the prompting of Harriet Stanton Blatch (daughter of Elizabeth Cady Stanton) and Alice Stone Blackwell (daughter of Lucy Stone), the NWSA and the AWSA merged into the National American Women's Suffrage Association (NAWSA). Stanton was its first president until Susan B. Anthony took over as president in 1892; Anthony was president until her resignation in 1900. The association itself, however, had a new, younger membership and was moving in a more conservative direction.

A More Conservative Approach

An example of this new conservatism was the NAWSA's willingness to compromise with southern legislators. In its efforts to win the vote in each state, the NAWSA distanced itself from controversial civil rights issues and played to the interests of the South by emphasizing educational requirements for voting. NAWSA members hoped that by advocating educational requirements as a prerequisite for voting, southern lawmakers would give the vote to predominantly white, educated women—rather than uneducated African American men.

A new generation of white women was obtaining higher education in greater numbers, entering professional careers, and earning respect as public speakers. But as far as the vote was concerned, they were still second-class citizens after five decades of struggle. The younger members of the suffrage movement were impatient with the lack of results. They felt that they deserved more rights, and they wanted them immediately. They watched as new male immigrants—some of whom did not speak English—received the right to vote on matters that would affect women. Yet these American-born women continued to be denied this right.

The new conservatism asserted its influence again when Stanton published her book, *The Woman's Bible*. The book was an indictment of Christianity and claimed it was the principal cause of women's oppression. Needless to say, this was a radical idea that caused a great deal of controversy. Since Stanton, one of the oldest and most prominent NAWSA members, wrote the book, the NAWSA was divided as to how to handle it. Despite arguments in its favor from Anthony, the majority of NAWSA members, led by Anna Howard Shaw, wanted to have nothing to do with the book.

Anthony and Stanton remained friends to the very end of their lives. Ideologically, however, they grew further and further apart over time. Anthony became more conservative while Stanton became more radical. Anthony remained an influential force in the NAWSA until she died. Under her conservative leadership, younger members of the organization moved toward a more pragmatic approach to winning the vote. They realized that unless they could engage a mainstream and more politically moderate population, they would always be looked upon with some suspicion. They did not want to be perceived as a minority group of women with radical ideas. While unwilling to discredit the achievements of pioneering suffragist leaders, they tried to soften their image in order to gain wider appeal. They needed an icon to symbolize their struggles, so they chose Susan B. Anthony to be their patron saint. It is no accident that when we honor the women's movement today, we often think of Susan B. Anthony before Elizabeth Stanton, despite the fact that their careers were contemporaneous and both were equally influential.

Toward the end of the nineteenth century, NAWSA members embarked on a concentrated effort to gain the support of the southern states. They developed a strategy that they thought would appeal to southern legislatures. They argued that by giving women the right to vote while maintaining educational and property qualifications, they would actually be helping to guarantee white supremacy. They tried to argue that allowing white women to vote would effectively shut out the economically disadvantaged African American population. But the southern states had their own plan to circumvent the Fourteenth and Fifteenth Amendments without giving white women an ounce of advantage. They instituted numerous requirements for suffrage, including an outrageous "grandfather" clause, which required a voter to show proof of a male relative who had voted in the 1860 presidential election! When the constitutionality of the grandfather clause was challenged, the Supreme Court upheld it, saying that the requirements were allowed as long as race was not the sole consideration for disallowing the vote.

Carrie Catt's Society Plan

When Anthony resigned her NAWSA presidency in 1900 at the age of eighty, she chose Carrie Chapman Catt as her successor. Catt was generally recognized as an exceptional organizer. She earned her reputation when a suffrage referendum in Colorado passed in 1894 under her leadership. When Catt resigned four years later because of her husband's illness, Anna Howard Shaw took over the helm. Unlike Catt, Shaw, who was president from 1904 to 1915, was a passionate speaker but had little administrative talent. Under her leadership, the organization lost some of its focus. Most historians agree this was a comparatively quiet period in the women's movement. Fortunately, Catt resumed leadership in 1915 when she came back from England with her husband.

During Catt's first tenure as president of the NAWSA, she instituted what became known as the Society Plan. As its name suggested, the plan involved getting wealthy society people to contribute to the movement. Catt herself had married a man who later became quite wealthy. Her social circle included other wealthy and influential women. Such women had wealth and social standing, and their participation provided the group with both money and respectability. The NAWSA also actively sought out the growing population of middle-class and professional women. It did not, however, seek the participation of the growing number of African American activists.

The NAWSA's push toward respectability proved to be a strategically smart move. Not only did its treasury swell but so did membership—increasing to over 117,000, an almost 900 percent increase from 1906 to 1910. Because of the

47

large monetary contributions the Society Plan brought in, most NAWSA members supported the strategy. But a few, including Harriet Stanton Blatch, felt that the movement had become too elitist. Blatch founded her own organization in 1907—the League of Self-Supporting Women, which later became the Women's Political Union.

Women's Clubs and Organizations in the Early Twentieth Century

Beyond the suffragist organizations, women had formed other clubs and societies to promote common interests. The idea of a women's club was not a new one. As far back as the Revolutionary War, there were ladies' associations that worked to help colonial armies in their war efforts. There were women's clubs that held literary discussions and others that worked toward civic improvements. The General Federation of Women's Clubs, however, which was the national organization of women's clubs, did not endorse women's suffrage until 1914.

One of the oldest women's clubs was New York City's Sorosis. What was different about this club was its feminist overtones. Many members were middle- and upper-class professional women who were not given due recognition by their professional male counterparts. By forming their own association, they could offer a "system of rewards, of recognition of merit in women." Sorosis not only supported women's suffrage but also sought to end discriminatory practices against working women.

The Progressive Era

Around 1900, a new political movement was born called the Progressive Movement. The birth of this movement coincided with the rising political consciousness of women. Instead of being associated with a specific organization, some women who participated in political activism wanted to do so by concentrating on specific social issues. There were plenty of issues in addition to suffrage—problems such as alcoholism, child labor, discriminatory work practices, and political corruption, to name a few. The Progressive Era, which lasted until the end of World War I, had a crucial influence on the success of the suffrage movement.

Progressivism flourished at a time when dramatic social changes were taking place in American society. The enormous influx of immigrants to cities and large-scale urban industrialization brought new problems. America had quickly changed from a relatively agrarian, or farming, nation into a country of big corporations that were accountable to no one. Unregulated capitalism was becoming the dominant social, political, and economic force. Reformers demanded that the government oversee the activities of the new industries. They felt that big industries had to be regulated so that they would not take advantage of their workers or consumers just to make profits for the owners. Furthermore, as big corporations began to win favors from politicians, political corruption became a serious problem. Reformers also wanted to eliminate child labor and institute compulsory education. They wanted to pass regulations that would safeguard public health.

During the Progressive Era, suffragists saw another opportunity to argue their cause, based upon the traditional duties of women to protect the home and children. One of the most prominent Progressives, Jane Addams, wrote an essay, "Why Women Should Vote." It linked the interests of Progressivism to the success of women's suffrage. Addams wrote, "[As] society grows more complicated it is necessary that woman shall extend her sense of responsibility to many things outside her own home if she would continue to preserve the home in its entirety." As urbanization took place, the individual household became less self-sufficient; people had far less control over many aspects of their lives, such as obtaining food or clothing, or maintaining sanitation. The function and welfare of households became increasingly dependent on outside services and facilities.

Progressives used evidence of these dramatic societal changes to address the antisuffragists' argument that the right to vote was outside the traditional domain of a woman's influence. They pointed out that the public and the private had become one. In order to wield any influence over her private environment, a woman must, as Addams stated, "bring herself to the use of the ballot . . . May we not fairly say that American women need this implement in order to preserve the home?"

The Antisuffragist Movement

An unexpected reaction to the suffrage movement was the development of a women's antisuffrage movement. It officially started in 1882, with the establishment of the Massachusetts Association Opposed to the Further

This 1910 cartoon from the *New York World* parodied both the suffrage and antisuffrage movements.

Extension of Suffrage to Women (MAOFESW). Those who were involved in antisuffragism were known as the "Antis."

These women were not necessarily believers in the notion that "a woman's place is in the home." Rather, the Antis supported a different form of feminist activism. They were against women's involvement in politics—not because it was, as some men put it, "unfit" for ladies, but because they felt political ambitions were incompatible with non-partisan public service. They felt strongly that affiliation with a political party was a hindrance to achieving social reforms because politicians were more responsive to neutral parties. They believed that social reform could be achieved entirely by politics-free endeavors.

In light of the pervasiveness of politics in every sphere of life, then as now, this seemed like a misguided argument at best and naive at worst. In the end, the antisuffragists did have a historical impact. They managed to delay the achievement of suffrage for women even further. Nevertheless, some feminist historians today are taking a second look at the women's antisuffrage movement for its relevance as an alternative form of nonpartisan political activism.

A Move Away from Conservatism

The suffrage movement grew more conservative at the beginning of the twentieth century. It increasingly became the domain of middle- and upper-class women. Harriet Stanton Blatch rejected this elitist direction. She wanted to infuse new energy into the suffrage movement by including women from across the socioeconomic spectrum. Blatch, who had married an Englishman, lived in England for twenty years before returning to the United States in 1902. While in England, she witnessed a more aggressive and militant style of activism under the leadership of Emmeline Pankhurst. Blatch was impressed by the political power of the working class in England. The organization that Blatch founded in the United States, the League of Self-Supporting Women, combined the talents of both educated and working-class women.

The militant approach used tactics that gained publicity, such as parades, picketing, and outdoor meetings. These women rejected the notion that they should not appear to threaten the existing social order. The new suffragists even called themselves "suffragettes," after their militant counterparts in Britain. In the process, women and men had to widen the old definition of femininity to include such "unladylike" activities.

Nowhere was this split between the old and the new suffragist more apparent than in Blatch and her pioneering mother, Elizabeth Cady Stanton. They openly disagreed over the issue of including working women in the movement. Stanton believed that more harm than good would result by giving the vote to uneducated women, but Blatch felt that these women knew more about many things that needed reform than their wealthier sisters.

Blatch carried nineteenth-century feminist sentiment into the twentieth century by organizing women's issues around the notion of work. She contended that women had always worked—but that their work was usually in the home, and therefore unpaid. She insisted that this did not make women's work any less valuable. She believed that work was the issue that should unite all women. Whether a woman was poor and worked in a factory or was wealthy and contributed her time to public service, both benefited society with their labor. Blatch also reminded professional women of the value of the working-class women in their lives. It was the labor of working-class women that allowed professional women the freedom to do the things they wanted. Blatch's vision was insightful and prophetic. Nearly a hundred years later, women are still struggling with balancing career and family, a problem Blatch thought was "insoluble—under present conditions—for the women of the people."

The Beginning of Militancy

A new leader emerged in the last decade of the suffrage movement: Alice Paul. Paul returned to the United States in 1910 after living in Britain for three years. Once back home, she found an energized movement for women's suffrage. Suffragists stood on street corners and spoke out to large crowds. They were able to draw crowds because it was considered a spectacle in those days to see a woman give a public speech. Activist women also opened suffragist newsstands, where they sold pamphlets, magazines, buttons, ribbons, and postcards to promote the cause. In 1910, Washington became the first state in fourteen years to pass a women's suffrage amendment.

While living in Britain, Alice Paul was also inspired by the militant tactics of Emmeline Pankhurst and the Women's Social and Political Union (WSPU). She became exasperated by the conservative methods of the NAWSA under the leadership of Anna Howard Shaw. Paul was impatient with the state-by-state approach that the NAWSA pursued and felt that the only way to succeed in getting the vote was through a federal amendment. Under the auspices of the NAWSA, she formed the Congressional Union (CU) with the help of Lucy Burns, whom she met while traveling in Scotland.

The day before President Woodrow Wilson's inauguration in 1913, Paul organized 5,000 women to parade down Pennsylvania Avenue. Enraged at the women's public display, the crowd spat at them, shouted obscene remarks, and attacked them with burning cigarette butts. The resulting press coverage delighted Paul, but the NAWSA disapproved of the CU's tactics. Eventually Paul and her supporters split from the NAWSA altogether and formed the Woman's Party, which later became the National Woman's Party (NWP).

Paul continued to use militant tactics to draw attention to women's causes. By the turn of the nineteenth century, the state-by-state approach had resulted in four western states giving women the vote—Wyoming in 1869, Utah in 1870, Colorado in 1893, and Idaho in 1896. The militants held whichever political party was in power responsible for the lack of action regarding the suffrage amendment. NWP members in these states were instructed to vote against whichever party was in power in all elections.

Other NWP members in eastern states were determined to make the Wilson administration accountable for its stance that gave states the final say on suffrage. They interrupted President Wilson's speeches over and over to make him support a federal amendment. The NWP employed methods of civil disobedience in the form of peaceful protests. The NWP was the first group to picket outside the White House to demonstrate their political beliefs. The United States entered World War I a few months after the picketing started. President Wilson's war message was, "We shall fight . . . for democracy, for the right of those who submit to authority to have a voice in their own government." Paul found this sentiment ironic in light of Wilson's position on women's suffrage.

A few months after the picketing started, the protesters were put in jail. While in prison, Paul went on a hunger strike to demand political prisoner status, but instead was forcibly fed. When over thirty NWP members picketed in protest of her abusive treatment, they, too, were arrested. When they joined Paul in a hunger strike, they, too, were fed forcibly. One of the suffragists in prison, Elizabeth McShane, wrote in her diary of the indignities she suffered: "Dr. Ladd came with a tube that looked like a hose and a pint of eggs and milk. He rammed it down so fast that I couldn't breathe. Then he poured food in rapidly. I gagged and the food came up as fast as it went down."

The women received unusually harsh treatment while in prison—they were beaten and thrown around, sometimes they were not even allowed to use the toilet, and their injuries went untreated. But this rough treatment not only strengthened their resolve to persist but also solidified their belief that women desperately needed the vote in order to receive fair treatment. Never before was their second-class status more evident than while they were in prison. The government finally relented because of public outcry and released all of the prisoners almost half a year after it had first started to arrest protesters.

President Wilson became convinced that the NWP was a group of militant radicals. He even went so far as to advise Carrie Catt of the NAWSA to distance her group from them. He also asked for a news blackout of the activities of NWP, thereby diminishing its effectiveness. As for the NWP, it was convinced that Wilson was a hypocrite. It kept the pressure on his administration to pass a federal amendment for women's suffrage, also known as the Anthony Amendment. The women who organized the NWP were mostly middle-class and educated, and they held fast to the ideal that America had a tradition of democracy. They saw women's suffrage as a natural extension of that democracy. But the government's silent sanction of their nightmare experience in prison left the NWP angry and disillusioned. Their continuing militancy gave the NWP an increasingly radical reputation, and they began to attract other groups of activists who were equally unhappy with the government.

Carrie Catt and the Winning Plan

When Carrie Catt took over the leadership of the NAWSA in 1915, she did several things. In contrast to Alice Paul's aggressive tactics to be seen and heard, Catt adopted a nonthreatening strategy. Her approach was called the front door lobby because of her determination not to alienate the Wilson administration. Also, rather than take a stand against the myriad social injustices of the day, Catt chose to focus solely on the issue of women's suffrage. The advantage of returning to this strategy was a conservation of resources. The front-door approach also minimized the chances of alienating potential supporters.

Catt rejected a militant approach and instead courted the favor of the Wilson administration. She did this by refusing to participate in the peace movement against World War I, which other suffragists like Paul and Jane Addams joined. Instead, Catt participated in the war effort. What further distinguished Catt from other suffrage leaders was her pragmatism. Catt told Jane Addams that although she was a lifelong pacifist, she nevertheless believed that using NAWSA resources against the war effort was like "throwing a violet against a stone wall." Privately, however, Catt supported Addams and her Woman's Peace Party (WPP).

As the United States became increasingly involved in the growing conflict, anyone who was not prepared to go to war or support the war effort was considered unpatriotic or pro-German. Antisuffragists, in particular, used this rhetoric against peace-loving suffragists. Eager to downplay these negative charges, Catt convened a meeting of the NAWSA in

February 1917 to propose that the organization support the national war preparedness campaign. This had the desired effect of getting a positive response from the Wilson administration, but it also provoked bitter recriminations from Catt's friends at the Woman's Peace Party—from which she was promptly thrown out.

In 1916, Catt adopted the Winning Plan at an emergency meeting of the NAWSA. She had just resumed the leadership of the organization about a year before and was dissatisfied with the direction the NAWSA was going. The strategy of winning suffrage via a state-by-state approach had been largely unsuccessful. Although at one time Catt had been a proponent of this strategy, she now saw that it was clearly not working. Without centralized leadership, resources would not be spent most efficiently. In spite of resistance, especially by Southern representatives who feared that the interests of their states would be usurped by a federal amendment, Catt, with the support of Shaw, succeeded in persuading the NAWSA to adopt the Winning Plan.

The Winning Plan was a secret strategy to mobilize suffrage activists in all the states to act quickly and at the same time. Instead of having states act independently, Catt devised a master plan and assigned a specific role to each state. The states were to carry these campaigns out all at once to get whatever suffrage rights they could for women, whether in local elections or state elections. The Winning Plan was intended to surprise antisuffragists with a sudden concentrated effort, which, if successful, would build enough momentum to then push ahead for a federal amendment.

Ahead of Her Time

In 1916, Jeanette Rankin became the first woman elected to Congress on a progressive Republican platform that called for suffrage for women. One of her first actions was to introduce a bill that would have granted women citizenship independent of their husbands. Additionally, she campaigned for prohibition, child welfare reform, an end to child labor, and against U.S. participation in World War I.

As it turned out, the timing of the NAWSA's new focus could not have been better. One of the most powerful enemies of the women's suffrage movement was the liquor industry. The liquor industry became an enemy of the suffragists when women started campaigning against the consumption of alcohol. When temperance societies forced the government to pass legislation against the manufacture and sale of alcohol, the liquor lobby turned its attention and resources to fighting prohibition, and away from fighting women's suffrage. As a result, one of the biggest barriers to women's suffrage was eliminated. In less than two years after adopting the Winning Plan, the Nineteenth Amendment was passed in Congress.

Ratification of the Nineteenth Amendment

The Nineteenth Amendment was passed in January 1918, by a narrow margin of one vote over the required two-thirds majority in the House of Representatives. The Senate, however, did not vote on it until September, where it was defeated by a narrow margin: two votes short of the required two-thirds majority. Another Senate vote took place in February 1919. This time the amendment was defeated by one vote. After two more tries, the Nineteenth Amendment finally passed the House in May 1919, and the Senate in June two weeks later.

However, the amendment still needed ratification by thirty-six of the forty-eight states. This would take time. Almost a year after the amendment passed—after several defeats in the South in the early 1920s and a challenge by antisuffragists against the Ohio ratification—there were thirty-five states that had ratified the amendment—just one more state was needed.

The suffragists selected Tennessee as the state most likely to ratify the amendment. They decided to put pressure on the governor of Tennessee to convene a special session of the House and Senate of the state legislature, which he did. The Tennessee Senate easily ratified the amendment. But the House did not meet to vote until several days later. There, it came down to one yes vote—given by the youngest member of the House, a man from an antisuffragist district who had in his pocket a letter from his mother imploring him to "be a good boy" and do the right thing. At last, almost seventy-five years after Seneca Falls, women had the vote.

4 Dawn of the Modern Era

While the issue of suffrage dominated the women's movement at the turn of the twentieth century, it was only one of many changes facing the "new woman." As much as the arguably unfeminine acts of protesting and picketing altered the prevailing definition of femininity, so too did new literature and fashion.

Kate Chopin's novel *The Awakening* was published in 1899 and dealt with the taboo subject of female adultery. Its heroine went through an inner transformation that reflected what many women were going through at the time. Like teenagers who start to recognize their own will and the power to assert that will, women tried new and freer ways of acting, such as smoking cigarettes or dressing in less restrictive ways. Sexual freedom was another integral part of the women's movement. Feminists advocated birth control and free love, as well as economic independence and independence from husbands.

Birth Control

The phrase "birth control" was coined by Margaret Sanger, who felt that women had the right to know how to control their own reproduction. At the time, the Comstock Law made both abortion and the dissemination of contraception devices illegal. The law adversely affected working-class, uneducated women the most. Many women died needlessly in childbirth or from botched abortions. Sanger herself witnessed the death of a woman who attempted a self-induced abortion. Along with other women reformers, she sought to distribute information to all women concerning contraception. Sanger established the American Birth Control League, which in 1942 became Planned Parenthood. In order to gain mainstream support and funding, she presented the use of contraceptives as a medical issue rather than a feminist one.

In defiance of the Comstock Law, Sanger opened the first birth control clinic in Brooklyn, New York, in 1916. The clinic passed out diaphragms and literature about birth control to five hundred women. But after just ten days, the New York City Police Department shut the clinic down, charging Sanger and her sister, Ethel Byrne, with the dissemination of "obscene" materials. Byrne was released after public protest, but Sanger was tried, convicted, and sentenced to a thirty-day jail term. Once released from prison, she was even more determined to amend the obscenity laws that prevented doctors from prescribing contraception. The Comstock Law was finally amended in 1929, but not until 1965, a year after Margaret Sanger's death, did the U.S. Supreme Court strike down the last remaining state law prohibiting the use of contraceptives.

Organizing for Change

Literary and other social clubs were formed to give women a forum where they could voice their ideas. One such club was the Heterodoxy Club, formed in 1912, which was the first public organization to provide a voice to lesbians. The Heterodoxy Club was unusual because no minutes of the meetings were kept. The reason for this was to promote the freest of thoughts without risk of censure. Furthermore, although club members were all professional women, their political orientations were diverse, which at times led to heated arguments.

In 1903, the Women's Trade Union League (WTUL) formed to fight for better working conditions for working-class women. WTUL organized work strikes and pickets against irresponsible employers who allowed dangerous working conditions, provided low wages, and required employees to work long hours. The need for this particular type of advocacy became most apparent when a deadly fire at New York City's Triangle Shirtwaist Company killed 146 people in 1911. The workers, mostly young female immigrants, were unable to flee the factory once the fire started because the company, ignoring safety regulations, had kept workers locked inside the factory.

The 1920s

The women's rights movement did not begin with suffrage, nor did it end with the passage of the Nineteenth Amendment. Women in the 1920s continued to be active in different social reform movements. The NAWSA became the League of Women Voters (LWV) in early 1919 and shifted its focus to educate and inform women on political issues. Still a nonpartisan organization, the LWV sought to ensure the benefits of democracy for all citizens. It pressed for legislation to eliminate all discriminatory practices against women and to protect the welfare of women and children. Today, the LWV continues to be relevant and is one of the sponsors of the presidential debates between the major candidates.

In 1921, the first piece of legislation resulting from women's votes was passed. The Sheppard-Towner Maternity and Infancy Protection Act used federal funds to support a preventative health care program designed to reduce maternal and infant mortality rates. American women could finally show the entire nation how their votes could make a difference. The new women voters worked hard to pass bills that mattered to them. Congressmen realized quickly that they could no longer ignore the interests of women, who were now half the voting population of the country.

The Sheppard-Towner Act encountered strong opposition from the American Medical Association (AMA), which was afraid that the government would now be able to dictate medical policy. In 1929, under increasing pressure from the AMA, funding for the program was finally stopped. However, the Sheppard-Towner Act did leave a positive legacy. Preventative health care, which had previously been unheard of, became an essential element of the services that physicians regularly provided.

At the same time, divisiveness among women's groups continued to undermine the effectiveness of women voters.

Young women in the 1920s enjoyed freedoms that the previous generation had fought to win.

In 1923, the National Women's Party (NWP) sponsored the Lucretia Mott Amendment, later to be known as the Equal Rights Amendment, which sought to obtain equality for all women and men. The fight to pass the ERA would continue for many decades. The ERA did not have the support of the NAWSA. The majority of NAWSA members believed that they had achieved what they had set out to do, and that the rest was up to the voters. In the end, 90 percent of NAWSA members resigned.

The Roaring Twenties also saw a new generation of young women enjoy freedoms that a previous generation had fought to win—freedoms that their mothers never had. It was the age of the flappers—young women whose provocative dress and behavior would have scandalized the public a decade earlier. There were few legislative changes in the 1920s; both child labor and minimum wage legislation failed to pass. Nevertheless, more women held public office at this point in history than ever before. Women also had more individual freedoms and educational and professional opportunities. More women than ever graduated from college and more went on to obtain post-graduate degrees.

The 1920s were also a time that saw an increase in the power of the political right. "Feminism" was considered by many to be a dirty word. The right portrayed feminists as frustrated man haters, or freakish spinsters. The Ku Klux Klan viewed feminism as a travesty of womanhood and an affront to patriotism.

Activists in the NWP argued for equality but were against the idea of treating women as a "special" group that needed special or protective laws. Social reformers, how-ever, wanted to pass such protective measures to ensure that working-class women would receive better working conditions, shorter working hours, and better wages. While the Women's Trade Union League (WTUL) united white working-class and middle-class women, it did not include African American women, who formed their own organization in 1920—the National Association of Wage Earners. The fight for equality in the workplace continues to be a relevant issue today.

The 1930s

The 1930s were the decade of the Great Depression. Suddenly women workers were seen as a threat because they were competing with men for the few jobs available. At this time, it was considered important for men to be the

Dynamic First Lady

She was the wife of President Franklin D. Roosevelt, but she won fame in her own right for her humanitarian work and as a role model for women in public life. As first lady, Eleanor Roosevelt broke many precedents. She held weekly press conferences with women reporters, lectured throughout the country, and hosted her own radio program. Traveling widely, she campaigned for measures to aid the underprivileged and racial minorities.

primary breadwinner for the family. When Franklin D. Roosevelt was elected president in 1932, he instituted the New Deal to stimulate demand for services and to create jobs. But because jobs were scarce, some states began to adopt discriminatory practices against married women workers. Women increasingly found that they had fewer opportunities. Furthermore, when work was available to them, they were being limited to unskilled clerical work and other traditionally female employment such as waitressing and laundering.

Social reformers had been trying unsuccessfully for over three decades to pass legislative reforms for minimum wages and maximum work hours. Each time these laws passed, the Supreme Court declared them unconstitutional. When the Roosevelt administration tried to pass

67

the National Industrial Recovery Act, it was struck down. Undaunted, the administration continued its efforts and sponsored the Fair Labor Standards Act, which was finally passed in 1938. The act established minimum wages and maximum working hours in industries involved in interstate commerce. It also prohibited the employment of anyone under sixteen. When the reformers finally won the minimum-wage legislation, they were dismayed to find that minimum rates for women were lower than those for men.

The decade also introduced new challenges to established notions of femininity. Ruth Benedict's *Patterns of Culture* in 1934 described a Native American society that was matrilineal and antiviolent. Margaret Mead's *Coming of Age in Samoa* also challenged traditional notions of gender roles. The book was a groundbreaking work in cultural and social anthropology, written after Mead's first trip to the Pacific Islands. It sparked debate regarding the influence of nurture and nature in social interaction and played a major role in the social and sexual revolution debates of the 1960s.

African American Women

In 1930, Jessie Daniel Ames, a member of the League of Women Voters, founded the Association of Southern Women for the Prevention of Lynching (ASWPL). It finally convinced Southern white women that it was time to take a stand against this barbaric and illegal practice. By Februrary 1937, eighty-one state, regional, and national organizations had endorsed the group's antilynching platform.

Before the 1930s, African American women exerted the greatest influence at the state and local levels. The most influential group of that time was the National Association of

Colored Women (NACW), which provided a network of resources for African American women. But in 1935, the National Council of Negro Women (NCNW) was organized to achieve changes in national policies. The moving force behind its foundation, Mary McLeod Bethune, had just accepted President Roosevelt's appointment as director of the Office of Minority Affairs of the National Youth Administration. She felt that the efforts of African American women had been previously diluted because these women lacked a unifying organization that provided focus and leadership. Bethune was the president of NCNW for fourteen years. Under her leadership, the organization lobbied for changes that improved the status of African American women as well as men.

The 1940s

The United States entered World War II in April 1941. This had a profound effect on the women's movement. In previous wars, women took jobs vacated by men as the men went off to war, but they did not venture too far from the domestic sphere. During the Civil War, women worked as nurses, cooks, and laundry women. During World War I, women replaced the men who worked in the factories. But it was during World War II that women had access to jobs in fields that had never been open to them before—as pilots, marines, coast guard members, welders, and electricians. By 1945, half of the workforce in the United States was female. Rosie the Riveter became the icon of the working woman who was contributing to the war effort.

Because of the desperate need for skilled labor, women suddenly were encouraged to learn new tasks and enter into new careers. More married women entered the workforce than ever before. Even though there was generally an unspoken understanding between men and women that this was only a temporary situation—after the war, "normal" gender roles would be resumed—the course was set for new definitions of femininity and new sexual identities for women to emerge. The paternalistic attitude that women needed men's protection was no longer acceptable.

Women in the Military

The government actively recruited women for military service—noncombative service only—by presenting the service as a glamorous, patriotic career choice. Women, however, were more than ready for new challenges and did not need much persuading. The military was an alternative to a very small set of choices available to most women at the time. Additionally, as more men went to war, there was an increase in the attendance of women at college, and an increase in the number of women in professional careers such as medicine, law, and banking.

Although the first bill to include women in the military was defeated, women pilots, led by Jackie Cochran, formed a civilian organization in 1942, the Women's Auxiliary Service Pilots (WASP). They entered into contracts with the Army Air Corps and did everything their male army counterparts did short of flying in combat. They lived under the same conditions as the men and performed the same dangerous task of testing problematic planes. In spite of their bravery, women pilots did not receive any military benefits, such as insurance or pension.

Before long, however, the armed services did start accepting women. The Women's Auxiliary Army Corps

(WAAC), which became the Women's Army Corps (WAC), was established in May 1942. The Navy established WAVES (Women Accepted for Volunteer Emergency Service) a few months later. Within six months, the Coast Guard and the Marine Corps both began to accept women. The fact that women had mostly noncombative duties effectively shut them out of the top command posts, however.

Racial discrimination continued to be a part of the military, as it was in society at large. African Americans, both men and women, were segregated from their white counterparts. And while white women in the army tended to be given clerical work, African American women more often than not worked in the kitchen. WAVES did not accept African American women until 1944, and then did so only because of pressure from President Roosevelt.

The late 1940s and the early 1950s saw Senator Joseph McCarthy's rise to power on the American political scene. McCarthy was an anti-Communist who conducted witch-hunts against all kinds of public figures for seven years beginning in 1947. American fear of Communism—the "Red Menace"—was an excuse for McCarthyites to persecute anyone, including many activists working for women's causes, under the cloak of "patriotism."

The 1950s

At the height of McCarthy's campaign of terror, it was a woman, Margaret Chase Smith, who had the courage and integrity to risk her career and reputation to speak out against McCarthy's persecutory tactics. Smith was the first woman

71

who was elected to both the House of Representatives and the Senate. Throughout her political career, she remained steadfastly true to what she believed to be right and became known as the "conscience of the Senate."

The 1950s were a time when women's organizations began to lose their momentum and focus. While suffrage had been achieved more than a generation earlier, there was still a need for numerous social reforms. But none of these reform movements had a goal as distinct as suffrage, nor did any enjoy the popular support of the suffrage movement. The Women's Trade Union League dissolved in 1950. The League of Women Voters was losing its members. The National Woman's Party continued to actively pursue the passage of the Equal Rights Amendment, but the ERA was defeated five times during the decade.

However, African American women remained active in the civil rights movement. One story that has become part of American mythology is the 1955 arrest of Rosa Parks in Montgomery, Alabama, which led to a yearlong boycott of the city's bus system. This was a time when Jim Crow laws that segregated African Americans from whites in all aspects of life were in effect everywhere. Parks, secretary of the local National Association for the Advancement of Colored People (NAACP), was arrested for refusing to move to the back of a segregated city bus. The boycott, called for by the local NAACP, was effective because of the efforts of the Women's Political Caucus, an organization of middle-class African American women. The buses remained empty for months, and civil rights leaders, including Dr. Martin Luther King Jr., regularly came to Montgomery to speak in community churches.

While women's organizations lost some momentum in the 1950s, African American women, like Rosa Parks, were active in the civil rights movement.

The NAACP challenged segregated education and won. The Supreme Court ruled in 1954 that segregation violated the Fourteenth Amendment. But it was not until a few years later in 1957 that the National Guard first escorted African American students to their white schools.

The 1950s were a decade of contradictions. On the one hand, there was greater prosperity; women had more freedoms than ever before. More women, including those who were married or mothers, worked outside of the home. But not all women who worked outside the home did so by choice. Many had to work out of necessity.

5 The Second Wave

During World War II, American women were encouraged to take jobs traditionally performed by men as a patriotic duty, and more than six million women did just that. As men fought the war, women operated heavy machinery, riveted, and welded. They built airplanes and ships for the war effort.

When men returned from the frontlines, American women were sent home from work. Imagine being told that you had to give up your job. What would you do if you were told that the "proper" thing for you to do was to get married and take care of your husband and children? Or that, if you worked, you were "stealing" a job from a man? These were some of the social pressures that women felt after World War II. Many women quit or were fired from their paying jobs and went home to raise families. Between 1945 and 1965, the baby boom generation was born—over 70 million babies.

Politically, the momentum of the women's movement was lost. Women no longer had a collective group identity or a shared sense of rights and responsibilities. Women occupied less than 5 percent of public offices. In 1952, the Women's Divisions of both the Democratic and Republican parties were eliminated.

The 1950s became a decade of conflicting messages for women. Fashion magazines and television shows like *Ozzie and Harriet* and *Leave It to Beaver* popularized the image of the happy housewife. In reality, however, a quiet revolution was taking place. Women—most of them married and in older age groups—reentered the workforce in large numbers. Women accounted for 60 percent of the growth in the labor force in the 1950s. They found jobs in the rapidly growing service sector as secretaries, nurses, waitresses, flight attendants, and clerks. These jobs were all considered to be appropriate for women. The new woman worker wanted to be recognized for her individual achievements, but she continued to receive the message that she was neglecting her most important responsibility: her family.

By the end of the 1950s, more women went on to higher education. The marriage and birthrates that created the baby boom generation began to slow down. When the United Auto Workers Women's Department ran workshops for women, they discovered a growing resentment about unequal pay. Unfair practices also kept women from advancing in their careers. But the women's rights movement was about to reemerge, renewed by widespread social changes that were taking place, particularly the growing civil rights movement and the introduction of the birth control pill.

Reproductive Rights

In 1960, the Food and Drug Administration (FDA) approved a new form of contraception: the birth control pill. The pill changed women's lives dramatically, mainly because they could now postpone or avoid bearing children. But it would take several years for public opinion to catch up with the freedoms promised by the pill.

Women still faced contradictory messages. The media warned young women that no man would marry them if they lost their virginity, while Masters and Johnson published groundbreaking scientific studies that proclaimed sexual satisfaction as the solution to a rising divorce rate.

The women's rights movement raised another important issue involving a woman's reproductive rights: the right to an abortion. Feminists insisted that the decision to end a pregnancy should belong to a woman, not to lawmakers or doctors. They insisted that it was a woman's right to own and control her body. Although abortion was illegal in the 1960s, some states permitted it if a woman's life was in danger. The danger, however, had to be proven and approved by a panel of doctors. Without other options, thousands of women resorted to illegal abortions each year. Usually performed by improperly trained people, these "back alley" abortions caused many deaths. Of the women who survived, many were infected, wounded, or left unable to bear children in the future. In the 1960s, feminists held public meetings where women could share their stories of illegal abortions. They lobbied to change antiabortion laws, which had been in existence since 1873.

Politics of Gender

A new wave of social change in the 1960s created a fresh forum for women's issues. While white, middle-class women struggled with their own social pressures, African American women and men faced racism and violence. The modern civil rights movement began in 1954, when the Supreme Court declared that school segregation—forced separation of blacks and whites—was unconstitutional. Throughout the 1950s and 1960s, African Americans continued to protest against discrimination and campaign for civil rights. They set an example for other minorities seeking reform. Women Strike for Peace, an organization of housewives and mothers, lobbied for a nuclear weapons test ban treaty. On college campuses, students protested the United States military's presence in Vietnam. Women played an important role in all these movements.

President's Commission on the Status of Women

In 1960, few people considered women's rights a priority. Even President John F. Kennedy, who regularly called for national change, appointed only nine women among his first 240 presidential appointments. Former first lady Eleanor Roosevelt was in her seventies at this time, but was still considered America's "most admired woman." When President Kennedy was elected, Roosevelt saw an opportunity to raise awareness for women's issues.

Women's Rights

Noticing that women were overlooked in the Kennedy administration, she sent the White House a list of women capable of holding top administrative posts. Around the same time, Esther Peterson, head of the Women's Bureau and assistant secretary of labor, approached Kennedy to establish a commission to investigate women's issues. Kennedy, who had won the election with much help from the female electorate, responded to Roosevelt and Peterson by creating the President's Commission on the Status of Women in 1961. Peterson, already the highest-ranking woman in his administration, became the committee's vice-chairperson. Eleanor Roosevelt chaired the commission until she became too ill; she died in 1962.

The commission issued a sixty-page report in 1963, entitled *American Women*, that opposed sex discrimination in jury service, marriage, and property rights. It called for equal pay, continuing education, vocational training, and social services for women. It also said that women should be considered for policy-making positions.

In response to the report, Kennedy issued a presidential order that required the civil service to hire for career positions "solely on the basis of ability to meet requirements of the position, and without regard to sex." The media gave the commission's report little coverage, but it nonetheless heightened consciousness among professional women. It also led to the creation of the Citizen's Advisory Council on the Status of Women to monitor these situations. Again influenced by Peterson, Kennedy approved of a plan for individual states to appoint their own commissions to investigate the status of women. Partly as a result of the work of the state commissions, many states changed laws affecting women in the workplace.

The Equal Rights Amendment Revisited

Meanwhile, a battle was taking place over the Equal Rights Amendment, which had been kept alive by the National Woman's Party since 1923. The ERA was an effort to eliminate discriminatory laws across the country, laws that denied women the right to serve on juries, barred them from certain kinds of jobs, and allowed husbands control over their wives and their wives' property. But in the 1920s, many women feared that the ERA would nullify important labor protections for women that had taken years to win.

The ERA's latest obstacle was the President's Commission on the Status of Women. Almost the entire commission, consisting of thirteen women and eleven men, opposed the amendment. They argued that the ERA was unnecessary since the Fifth and Fourteenth Amendments to the Constitution already guaranteed all citizens equal protection under the law. For her part, Peterson also worried that if the ERA passed, it would hurt the protective labor laws that were in place. The commission succeeded in delaying action on the ERA.

Another result of the commission's report was passage in 1963 of the Equal Pay Act, the first federal law to help women fight sex discrimination in the courts. It provided equal pay for men and women in jobs requiring equal skill, responsibility, and effort. The Equal Pay Act was an important turning point, although in practice, it was—and continues to be—difficult to determine what constitutes "equal" skill, responsibility, and effort.

The Feminine Mystique

Also in 1963, Betty Friedan, who would become a high-profile figure in the women's movement, published *The Feminine Mystique*. Friedan had lost her newspaper job after requesting a second period of maternity leave. She identified the anxiety and discontent felt by women of her generation as the "feminine mystique." She wrote: "If a woman had a problem in the 1950s and 1960s, she knew that something must be wrong with her marriage, or with herself . . . She was so ashamed to admit her dissatisfaction that she never knew how many other women shared it. If she tried to tell her husband, he didn't understand what she was talking about. She did not really understand it herself."

The best-selling book stressed the need women had for an identity that was outside the home and marriage. Friedan heightened awareness of the obstacles women faced in seeking fulfillment. Women were powerless in both family and society. They had few opportunities for self-expression beyond the roles of caregiver, consumer, and sexual icon. Women seeking careers encountered these negative stereotypes as well as discrimination in the form of unequal salaries and limited opportunities for growth. Friedan blamed the media, educators, sociologists, and psychologists for propagating myths of female domesticity. At the same time, she did not want women to be seen as helpless victims. Friedan advocated increased education and career opportunities for women. In response, thousands of women from around the country wrote to thank her for giving their unhappiness a name.

The Feminine Mystique became a unifying force in this second wave of the women's movement.

The Civil Rights Act

Working-class women and African American women had to contend with their own issues. African American women had long been in the workforce but remained in menial and segregated jobs. The 1963 Equal Pay Act excluded farm and domestic workers, so for many black women, the passage of the act was meaningless. Throughout the 1960s, the wages of black women fell short of those of white women, who themselves were only making about 60 percent of what white men earned. African American women like Ruby Doris Smith, who became a political leader, played an important role in the struggle to end all types of discrimination.

In the electrically charged, racist South, Fannie Lou Hamer risked death when she raised her hand during a drive to register black voters. Soon afterward, she went to a Mississippi courthouse to register her vote. She was fired from her job, her house was bombed, and she was thrown off the land she had sharecropped for years. Undaunted, she joined the Student Nonviolent Coordinating Committee to help others register to vote. In 1964, 63,000 black voters were registered in Mississippi. The same year, Hamer even ran for Congress.

In 1964, Title VII of the Civil Rights Act made employment discrimination on the basis of race, religion, and national origin illegal. At the last minute, the category of sex discrimination was included, in spite of opposition. Many

81

liberals were worried that this addition would make the bill appear laughable. Representative Martha Griffith pointed out that anyone who doubted that women were second-class citizens need only listen to the ridicule coming from the men. Nevertheless, Title VII became the strongest legal tool for women to date. Title VII of the Civil Rights Act was followed by Executive Order 11246, which made it illegal to discriminate on the basis of race, color, religion, sex, or national origin in hiring for federally contracted work.

The Equal Employment Opportunity Commission

After the Civil Rights Act was passed, the Equal Employment Opportunity Commission (EEOC) was established to investigate complaints of discrimination. For example, airlines still fired stewardesses who married or turned thirty-two, and newspapers still advertised jobs for men and women in separate columns. Of the EEOC's five appointees—selected by Lyndon Johnson, who became president after Kennedy's assassination in 1963—only one, Aileen Clarke Hernandez, was a woman. As Hernandez noted, "the commission was not planning to be an example to industry of the meaning of 'equal opportunity employer.'"

It quickly became clear that the EEOC's priority was race discrimination, especially as it related to African American men. Although the EEOC received 50,000 sex discrimination complaints in its first five years, it took few steps to follow up on them. They were widely considered to be something of a joke. The *New York Times* referred to it as the "bunny law," a reference to *Playboy* magazine, which first hit the newsstands in 1953, and its Playboy bunnies. The *Times* editors wondered what would happen if a man applied for a job as a Playboy bunny and was rejected. Could he charge discrimination?

Among the complaints sent to the EEOC were those concerning state laws. Some of these prohibited women from working in certain occupations, limited the number of hours they could work, and set a separate minimum wage for them. In upholding an Oregon law that limited the number of hours a woman could work, the Supreme Court's decision stated that a "woman's physical structure and the performance of maternal functions place her at a disadvantage in the struggle for subsistence . . . [she] is properly placed in a class by herself." Women saw these so-called protective labor laws, which regulated their employment, less as protective measures and more as obstacles to better job opportunities and pay. They raised the issue that these state laws were in conflict with Title VII. In November 1965, the EEOC released guidelines to cover these complaints. The guidelines supported the state laws provided that "the employer is acting in good faith and that the law in question is reasonably adapted to protect women rather than to subject them to discrimination."

NOW

In 1966, a group of delegates to the third National Conference of State Commissions on the Status of Women, including Betty Friedan, submitted a resolution to the conference. The resolution condemned the EEOC's refusal to deal with sex discrimination complaints. To their dismay, the conference refused to allow it. This convinced Friedan and the others that, even with the state commissions and federal agencies, women still had no effective voice in government. As it was, Friedan and the other women were frustrated with the attitude of women's organizations such as the League of Women Voters. Fearing the label "feminist," the organizations refused to protest against sex discrimination or lobby for the enforcement of Title VII.

Thus, the twenty-eight frustrated women founded the National Organization for Women (NOW). Friedan became its first president. Within a few months, its charter members numbered 300 men and women. Its first board was made up of university professors and administrators, labor union officials, government officials, business executives, and one medical doctor. NOW's stated purpose was to "take action to bring women into full participation in the mainstream of American society now, assuming all the privileges and responsibilities thereof in truly equal partnership with men." One of its immediate goals was to see Title VII enforced.

In 1967, Friedan presented a bill of rights at the organization's second annual convention, demanding paid maternity leave, educational aid and job training, and tax deductions for child care. The bill of rights also demanded legalized abortions and passage of the ERA, two controversial issues that would alienate many of NOW's members. Over the years, NOW would struggle with its definition of women and its own agenda. It has been criticized for

The National Organization for Women (NOW) was founded in 1966 by women frustrated with the League of Women Voters and other groups that refused to protest against sex discrimination. Currently, NOW is the largest organization of feminist activists in the United States.

views that were perceived by the majority of American women as too extreme; for having "nothing to say to the average American woman"; for being too militant; for being too conservative; and for being too narrow in focus. Yet these criticisms would not stop NOW from becoming the nation's largest and most powerful women's organization. NOW has 500,000 contributing members and 550 chapters in all fifty states. NOW's mission remains taking action to bring about equality for all women.

6 Grass Roots and Beyond

In 1968, a group of radical women protested the Miss America beauty pageant in Atlantic City by crowning a sheep the winner. They threw high-heeled shoes, bras, girdles, and magazines like *Playboy* and *Cosmopolitan* into a trash can, calling them "instruments of torture to women." They were forever ingrained in the public's imagination as "bra-burners." But they set the stage for more radical approaches to feminism. While NOW had been established to fill the gap left by groups like the League of Women Voters, it and similar organizations were being rejected by younger, more radical women.

Inspired by the civil rights movement, young activists organized and formed groups to oppose the Vietnam War. They attracted women in hundreds of communities. They addressed the needs of different groups of women, including lesbians, ethnic minorities, and welfare recipients, and concentrated on raising awareness of issues that affected their everyday lives. They met other women who shared their frustrations and hopes, leading to a new feminism that grew on a grassroots level and addressed personal issues. Many of the victories of the 1970s dealt with issues such as getting husbands to help with housework, long-awaited promotions at work, and gathering the financial and emotional resources to leave an abusive partner.

Grassroots projects helped establish women's newspapers, bookstores, and cafés. Crisis hotlines and women's shelters were created for the first time to support victims of sexual and domestic abuse. Until the 1970s, inadequate laws made it difficult to convict those accused of rape. The burden of proving sufficient resistance was placed on the victim. Conservative social attitudes toward women's sexuality and behavior made this a near impossible task.

Women also found the language that was used to describe gender and gender roles to be woefully obsolete. New attitudes developed into a new vocabulary. The phrase "women's lib," or women's liberation, became common, and "sisterhood" described female unity. The debate over whether women and men were essentially different or the same led to the use of "Ms." instead of "Miss" or "Mrs." New feminist scholarship touched on almost every discipline, leading colleges and universities to introduce women's studies programs. These programs taught culture and history from a woman's perspective.

Ms. Magazine

Called a "passing fad," Ms. magazine, the first feminist mass-market magazine in history, was founded by several

Ms. magazine, the first mass-market feminist magazine, provided a forum for many feminist writers.

activists, most notably Gloria Steinem. It was published in 1971 as a one-time insert in *New York* magazine; 300,000 copies were sold. Its first solo issue was published the next year. *Ms.* published articles that kept the national debate on women's identity alive—advocating the ERA and pioneering the idea of raising children without sex roles. It gave voice to many feminist writers, including Barbara Ehrenreich and Susan Faludi. Future Pulitzer Prize winner Alice Walker was an early contributor to *Ms.*

"A Watershed Year"

Congresswoman Bella Abzug called 1972 "a watershed year" for passing women's rights legislation. As she put it, "There was no opposition. Who'd be against equal rights for women?" More and more rallies and demonstrations were being held for women's rights. Lawmakers responded to women, who made up a large percentage of the voting public, leading to legal victories for women's rights.

In 1972, Congress passed Title IX of the Higher Education Act, providing women equal access to higher education and to professional schools. It opened the doors to women in the fields of medicine, law, engineering, and other professions. But nowhere was its success more clear than in the arena of women's athletics. In the mid-1970s, one in twenty-seven high school girls played sports; today that number is one in three. Subsequently, women staked their claim in the Olympic Games, taking home gold, silver, and bronze medals year after year.

Congress Approves the Equal Rights Amendment

The ERA finally passed Congress in 1972. Before that, support for the ERA had been increasing; the League of Women Voters, Business and Professional Women, the YWCA, the American Association of University Women, Common Cause, and the United Auto Workers all now supported the ERA. Polls showed that a nationwide majority supported it. Finally, on March 22, the Equal Rights Amendment was approved by Congress and sent to the states for ratification before it could be written into the Constitution. The ERA stated: "Equality of rights under the law shall not be denied or abridged by the United States or by any state on account of sex."

Despite the victories, there were still very few women in state legislatures to vote in support of the ERA. Its passage was in the hands of male lawmakers. Meanwhile, the media gave much coverage to the opponents of the ERA. Opponents argued that it would give the government too much control over the private lives of citizens, and charged that it would lead to women being drafted, as well as gay marriages and unisex toilets. When the deadline for state ratification came in 1982, it fell three states short of the thirty-eight needed. Although 75 percent of the women lawmakers in those three states supported the ERA, only 46 percent of the men did.

Roe v. Wade

Since the 1960s, women had demonstrated and lobbied lawmakers to change abortion laws. In 1973, when the

Supreme Court handed down its decision in the landmark case *Roe v. Wade*, it appeared that even on this controversial point, feminists were unstoppable.

Jane Roe was a pseudonym for a single, pregnant woman in Dallas County, Texas. She had brought a federal suit claiming that the Texas law that made abortion a criminal act was unconstitutional and abridged her personal privacy by denying her the right to a medically safe abortion. She sued "on behalf of herself and all other women" in the same situation. In a seven-to-two ruling, the Supreme Court ruled that the Sixth Amendment gave a woman the right to decide whether or not to have an abortion. Although public opinion supported the idea that abortion was a private concern and not a matter of public policy, the Court's ruling propelled into action a staunch minority opposed to abortion.

Antiabortion groups formed with the support of the Catholic Church and fundamentalist Christian groups. They had several legal victories, including the Hyde Amendment to the Health, Education, and Welfare Appropriations Bill. The amendment, which passed in 1976, prevented the use of federal funds for abortions, except in cases where the mother's life was endangered. Supporters argued that abortion should not be funded by taxpayers, many of whom considered it to be immoral. Critics of the amendment called it unconstitutional and discriminatory, since the absence of legal abortions affected poor women and women of color above all. Abortion continues to be the most emotional and divisive issue on the feminist agenda.

The New Black Feminism

For many African American women, racial, not sexual discrimination, was the main source of oppression. Although the women's rights movement of the 1960s and 1970s intended to speak for all women, it was largely seen as a movement for white middle-class women. Black feminist ideas were inspired by the experiences of ordinary black women. They felt that sexism was only one part of the problem and stressed the necessity of continued work with black men against class oppression and racism.

African American women had long been active in the pursuit of civil rights. Since the 1890s, they had formed women's clubs in support of social welfare or education projects. Throughout the 1960s and 1970s, the National Association of Colored Women (NACW), formed in 1896, shifted focus from mainly civil rights concerns to the problems of women in general and minority women in particular. Poor African American women challenged the discriminatory practices of the welfare system and formed the National Welfare Rights Organization to get more benefits for eligible women and children. In 1975, the National Council of Negro Women (NCNW) prepared a report on the status of women in housing, documenting the problems women faced "when they try to acquire and maintain a decent place to live." It received a grant to study the NCNW programs designed to alleviate poverty in Mississippi.

Newer groups followed in the footsteps of the NCNW. Founded in 1970, the Coalition of 100 Black Women develops programs to deal with a range of issues faced by black women. In 1973, the National Black Feminist Organization was established. In 1971, Congresswoman Shirley Chisholm joined Bella Abzug and Betty Friedan to form the National Women's Political Caucus. Its goal was to make women more visible in politics. Chisholm became the first black member of Congress in 1969. At the time, only ten women and eight African Americans were members of the House of Representatives. Before her retirement in 1983, she achieved a number of firsts, including being the first African American to run for the presidency in 1972.

Women in the Military

In higher education, only U.S. service academies still refused to admit women in the early 1970s. In 1974, the Department of Defense supported an official statement issued by the Departments of the Army, Navy, and Air Force against the admission of women to their academies. They argued that since women were barred from combat, they did not need the expensive training offered at military academies such as West Point. They feared that women would threaten the traditions of the academies and that they would simply not meet the demanding standards.

Supporters of making the academies coeducational argued that women should have the same access to the training needed to rise in their military careers. After all, they were free to pursue all but three of twenty-four career fields in the military. In 1975, the House of Representatives passed the Stratton Amendment, which called for the admission of women into the academies. The following year, 119 women matriculated at the Military Academy, 81 at the Naval Academy, and 157 at the Air Force Academy.

The story of Karen Silkwood, a worker who exposed radioactive hazards at an Oklahoma plutonium processing plant, provided the basis for a 1983 film starring Meryl Streep.

This did not change the opinion of many men in the military that the admission of women was a mistake.

The Workplace

Increasingly, women entered careers that had been traditionally reserved for men. As a result, issues of gender were pushed to new boundaries. For example, in 1979, NOW took up a case of workplace sex discrimination involving a female firefighter who was prohibited from breast-feeding her baby at work during her time off. Working women also raised workplace safety issues. Karen Silkwood exposed radioactive hazards at the plutonium-processing plant where she worked. After her death in a mysterious car accident, NOW kept up pressure for an inquiry into the plant hazards. In 1979, a court found the Oklahoma company liable for plutonium contamination and ordered it to pay damages of $10.5 million. The story became the basis for the movie *Silkwood*, starring Meryl Streep.

Rising divorce rates made many women the heads of their households. But divorce often left women poor because of reduced awards for alimony and the burden of having to raise children alone. Meanwhile, many women were stuck working in low-paying jobs. In the mid-1970s, an economic boom was replaced with rising inflation. As real wages for all workers declined, those of women fell even further. Women found it more difficult than ever before to support a family alone. Faced with job and financial insecurities, both men and women took another look at the issues of gender equality, and an antifeminist backlash grew.

The Congressional Caucus for Women's Issues

In 1977, fifteen women then in Congress founded the Congressional Caucus for Women's Issues (CCWI) in order to advance a legislative agenda to benefit women. Immediately, they met to discuss social security and private welfare reform, as well as child care and job training to get women off of welfare programs. In spite of its low membership—representing just 10 percent of the House of Representatives at its peak—the Caucus has had many successes over the years. The year 1993, when twenty-four women were elected to Congress, doubling the Caucus's membership, was called the "Year of the Woman."

The Caucus's first legislative package was the Economic Equity Act (EEA), which over the years has addressed many women's issues, including health insurance coverage for dependents, child support, and tax and retirement policies. It has also led efforts to improve women's health and protect victims of domestic violence and sexual assault. Its victories include the Family and Medical Leave Act. Women both inside and outside of Congress spent eight years campaigning for the passage of this bill, which gives an employee the right to take leave from work to care for a sick family member without fear of losing his or her job. The Women's Health Equity Act has brought billions of additional dollars to women's health research and services.

In 1995, the House of Representatives voted to eliminate funding for staff and offices of caucus organizations.

The CCWI lost its right to have office space in the congressional building and to collect membership dues from members of Congress. The CCWI reorganized under the same name, continuing to promote an agenda for women. Its membership now includes fifty-six women. Its current agenda includes bills that deal with violence against women, women's health, equal opportunity, education, child care, retirement, veterans, and women in business.

7 A Decade of Transition

After a decade of notable achievement for the women's rights movement, the 1980s must have seemed to many feminists a decade of backlash. Susan Faludi, author of *Backlash: The Undeclared War Against American Women*, wrote that throughout history, backlashes to women's advancement were triggered by the public perception that women had made great progress, whether or not they actually had. Just when women seemed closest to closing the gender gap, they were perceived as a threat and their efforts struck down.

In the 1980s, "postfeminism" became a common term, used to describe the attitudes of a younger generation of women—an attitude that included an indifference to the struggles and aims of their predecessors. Women entered business and professions with optimism. Two-income professional families generated a new, high-consumption standard of living. Meanwhile, the media convinced the public that sexual equality had been achieved, supported by successful, visible women who seemed to "have it all."

But were real women's prospects really that good? As Faludi points out, in the 1980s, women represented two-thirds of all poor adults; nearly 75 percent of full-time working women made less than $20,000 a year; nearly 80 percent of working women were still stuck in traditional "female" jobs as secretaries, salesclerks, and administrative support workers; and only two of the *Fortune* 500 chief executives were women. At home, women continued to do 70 percent of the household duties. Divorced fathers paid 25 percent less in child support than they had in the 1970s. Women's reproductive freedom was in greater jeopardy than a decade earlier. And in the late 1980s, domestic violence was the leading cause of injury to women.

Feminists themselves became increasingly divided over what their agenda should include. They argued over the definition of feminism and its goals. Social feminists centered the debate on class conflict. Liberal feminists stressed the importance of equal rights legislation. Radical feminists waged battles around the politics of the body. Feminists like Sheila Rowbotham also point to the administration of President Ronald Reagan (1981–1989) as responsible for putting the ERA, as well as civil rights, abortion, and social welfare, on the back burner. Certain conservative groups blamed feminists for everything, from higher divorce rates to job shortages.

The ERA Is Defeated

In 1982, in spite of the tremendous campaign in support of it, the Equal Rights Amendment was defeated. Opponents of the amendment had spread the idea that it would bring about changes in gender identity. Phyllis Schlafly, founder of STOP ERA, predicted that eighteen-year-old girls would be drafted, abortion would be federally funded, and homosexual marriages would be legalized. Opposition to the ERA revived right-wing politics and united conservative groups, which included women like Teddi Holt, who as a "homemaker and a Christian mother" felt threatened by the feminist movement. The ERA was reintroduced in 1983, but it was not passed.

The Antiabortion Backlash

The main issue that conservative groups united around in the 1980s was abortion. They responded to the successes NOW activists had achieved in defeating antiabortion bills introduced into state legislatures. In 1983 alone, almost one hundred antiabortion bills were introduced, but fewer than twenty passed. Meanwhile, antiabortion groups continued the aggressive tactics begun in the late 1970s, gathering outside clinics to protest and to harass the women entering them.

The antiabortion fervor grew into a pattern of violence against women's health clinics and personnel. In May 1983, after ten years of weekly picketing, an arsonist set fire to the Hillcrest Clinic in Norfolk, Virginia. The vice president of the Virginia Society of Human Life told the press that "we rejoice" at the news of the fire. Damages totaled approximately $140,000. The antiabortion group Army of God claimed responsibility and threatened that this was only the beginning.

In the 1980s, NOW activists successfully defeated many antiabortion bills introduced into state legislatures, prompting a backlash from antiabortion activists.

The following year saw a peak in violence against clinics where abortions were performed. Joseph M. Scheidler, director of the Pro-Life Action League, published the book *Ninety-Nine Ways to Close the Abortion Clinics*. The book gave tips on how to intimidate and terrorize women entering clinics. Scheidler boasted that complications for patients increased 4 to 5 percent on the days that the group protested outside.

Around the country, clinics were torched or bombed. In Birmingham, Alabama, two men entered a clinic during office hours and ran through the facility destroying equipment with an industrial sledgehammer. The headquarters of the National Abortion Federation in Washington, DC, was bombed. Supreme Court Justice William Brennan, who authored the 1973 *Roe v. Wade* decision that legalized abortion, received a death threat from the Army of God.

In 1985, the antiabortion faction tried a different tactic, releasing a factually inaccurate and highly emotional film called *The Silent Scream*. Segments of this antiabortion film, which told an allegedly true story of an abortion performed at eleven weeks after conception, were aired on network television. Alarmed by the terrorist attacks, NOW chapters all over the country conducted around-the-clock vigils in thirty abortion clinics in eighteen states over one weekend and continued providing escort services for patients entering clinics throughout 1985. The following year, NOW president Eleanor Smeal announced that the organization would file civil suits in federal courts against the attackers of abortion clinics.

In court, battles over abortion rights were hard-fought. In *Thornburgh v. American College of Obstetricians and Gynecologists* (1986), the U.S. Supreme Court stated for the first time that "a woman's right to make that choice freely is fundamental." The importance of *Roe v. Wade* could not be made louder or clearer than it was in Arkansas in November 1988, where the antiabortion faction successfully amended the state constitution to define life as beginning "at conception." If *Roe v. Wade* were reversed, this amendment would immediately make abortion illegal in Arkansas. Organizations like NOW had to keep a vigil against the forces that sought to reverse *Roe v. Wade*.

NOW in the 1980s

In the face of opposition resulting from increased visibility, feminists continued to take a stand. During the 1980s,

NOW's membership grew to 165,000. NOW chapters around the country took active roles in a wide range of issues, from the fight for reproductive rights to the arrest and prosecution of rapists. They pursued new legislation for the collection of child support payments and for lesbian and gay rights.

The NOW Legal Defense and Education Fund filed lawsuits on behalf of individuals and women at large. In 1984, it brought a $2 million lawsuit against Mutual of Omaha, the largest provider of individual health and disability insurance in the country, charging that the company's insurance prices were higher for women than men.

A 1986 *Newsweek* poll gave feminism high marks. It showed that 56 percent of all American women considered themselves feminists. Seventy-one percent believed that the feminist movement had helped them, and only 4 percent considered themselves antifeminist. Perhaps Eleanor Smeal, former president of NOW, summed it up best: "Not a moment of it was wasted, even if we never win."

Gay and Lesbian Rights

While women fought for their rights as a group, they served as an example to gays and lesbians, who also face sex discrimination. Lesbians have felt silenced and left out even in women's rights organizations. They found a voice only within radical feminist groups, in which they began to develop a lesbian feminist perspective.

Lesbians also share a community with gay men, who have traditionally been more vocal in their pursuit of equal treatment. The Stonewall Rebellion of 1969 is widely regarded as the birth of the modern gay and lesbian liberation movement. In June of that year, the police entered the Stonewall Inn in New York City, allegedly to look for violations of the alcohol control laws. They threw patrons, most of whom were gay, out of the bar, inciting a riot. From the Stonewall Rebellion onward, gays and lesbians fostered a strong group identity. Gay organizations were founded and marches were organized to commemorate Stonewall each year.

Gays and lesbians often face the same kind of marginalization and discrimination as women. However, they also confront unique issues. Thus, organizations exclusively for gay men and lesbians have been formed. In 1977, the National Center for Lesbian Rights, a feminist, progressive legal center, was created to tackle such issues as AIDS discrimination, gays and lesbians in the military, media images of gays and lesbians, child custody for gay parents, same-gender marriages, and domestic partnerships.

In 1985, the Gay and Lesbian Alliance Against Defamation (GLAAD) was formed in protest against sensational stories about AIDS published in the *New York Post*. The founders of GLAAD saw the need for a media watchdog to educate the media and entertainment industry, as well as the public, about homosexuality. GLAAD's ultimate goal is to end antigay and antilesbian violence and discrimination. In 1987, the National Gay and Lesbian Rights March drew 500,000 protesters to Washington, DC, more than five times the number who attended the 1979 lesbian and gay rights march.

Despite discrimination and sexual harassment, women continued to be integrated into the military during the 1980s.

Women in the Military, Part Two

In the 1980s, women continued to be integrated into the military, in spite of efforts to thwart their progress. In 1983, the United States Coast Guard began to integrate women completely. The top "midshipman" in the U.S. Naval Academy's class of 1984 was a woman, the first to graduate at the head of the class at a service academy since women were admitted in 1976. Kristine Holdereid's class standing was based on both academic grades and marks in military performance.

In 1987, the air force struck down the last restriction on the assignment of women officers to nuclear missile crews, which required that women be teamed with other women on the two-person crews serving at the controls of missiles. That same year, the navy announced that it would open a wide range of new jobs to women and would increase efforts to combat sexual harassment against female sailors. Although this policy opened about 10,000 posts aboard logistics ships and some aircraft to enlisted women and officers, it was designed to keep women out of combat. The study on which these changes were based also disclosed that sexual harassment was the most common complaint from women sailors.

As women began to make gains in the military, complaints of sexual harassment and rape also rose. In 1987, the Executive Committee of the Defense Advisory Committee on Women in the Services reported on "abusive behavior" and "blatant sexual harassment" in both the navy and marines. These culminated in the much-publicized 1991 Tailhook Association Convention scandal, which brought the public's attention to sexual harassment in the military.

The New Working Woman

Complaints to the Equal Employment Opportunity Commission of sex discrimination and sexual harassment in the workplace increased by nearly 25 percent in the 1980s. In an economic climate that included a recession and an increase of minimum-wage service jobs, women were more likely than men to lose their jobs or have their wages cut. Feminist author Susan Faludi notes that in 1986, women working full-time made only 64 cents to a man's dollar—the same gap that working women faced in 1955.

This inequity led to record numbers of sex discrimination suits and landmark rulings in favor of women. In 1983,

First In Space

Dr. Sally Ride became the first American woman in space on the shuttle *Challenger*'s 1983 mission. An advocate for improved science education, Ride has written three children's books, *To Space and Back, Voyager: An Adventure to the Edge of the Solar System*, and *The Third Planet: Exploring the Earth from Space*. Dr. Ride is currently a member of the President's Committee of Advisors on Science and Technology, and professor of physics at the University of California, San Diego.

a federal district judge ordered the state of Washington to pay an estimated $838 million in raises and back pay to women in predominantly "female" jobs who were being paid 20 to 30 percent less than men in similar jobs. This encouraged future wage discrimination suits.

Yet, while women made strides in courts of law during the 1980s, working women lost ground in the courts of popular opinion. Best-sellers like *Smart Women/Foolish Choices, If I'm So Wonderful, Why Am I Still Single?* and *Women Men Love/Women Men Leave* asserted that women had sacrificed happiness for independence. Popular psychologists used feminist-sounding rhetoric to peddle their advice. They urged women to "get power" by "surrendering and submitting" to men's every whim.

In spite of the declining economic power of women, the media falsely reported that the wage gap was closing. The EEOC claimed that sexual harassment in corporate America was falling, although its own figures showed the contrary. Meanwhile, the Reagan administration cut the EEOC's budget in half, forcing it to cut back dramatically the number of sex discrimination suits it pursued.

8 New Issues, Old Issues

In spite of the legislative victories of the last four decades, feminists continue to struggle with the sexual division of society. As sociologist Rose-Marie Lagrave wrote, "Despite the growing feminization of society, the contest between men and women remains too unequal for any genuine competition to take place." How much has the condition of women really improved? Has it improved because the gap between men and women has closed or because of other factors, such as economic growth and the improved condition of men? In other words, is the progress made by women still tied to the condition of men?

To assess the progress of American women, let us take a look at education. Between 1973 and 1994, women's share of postgraduate degrees increased dramatically, jumping by 52 percent for bachelor's degrees, 77 percent for master's degrees, and 481 percent for professional degrees, which include dentistry, law, and medicine. By the mid-1990s, more women than men aged twenty-five to thirty-five had earned at least a bachelor's degree.

The good news is that the doors of education are now wide open to women, and education increases earning power. On closer inspection, however, the inequality between the sexes has not been eliminated. Inequality emerges in new forms. The problem, as Lagrave put it, is not that too few girls have the chance to earn an education, but that schools reproduce existing differences between the sexes and fail to prepare female graduates for the realities of the marketplace.

Women choose already "feminized" areas of study, such as languages, literature, and education. Their increased representation in education hides the fact that the diplomas they receive are worth less than in the past and that their professional opportunities are limited, Lagrave said. Far fewer women than men enter such disciplines as engineering and physical sciences, which lead to highly skilled and therefore higher-paying jobs. Of all doctoral degrees awarded in the United States in 1994, 20 percent went to men in the field of engineering, compared with 4 percent to women in the same field.

With much work still to be done, what is the current state of the women's rights movement? "Feminism, in the sense of a historical movement calling for social transformation, is no longer in vogue," writes Francoise Thébaud, editor of *A History of Women*. Although debate over the issues remains, the days of demonstrations and organized collectives seem to have passed. However, the current state of feminism may illustrate one of the greatest achievements of the second wave of the women's rights movement: to bring about a society in which it is no longer needed. No longer does society have to be reminded to take women and women's issues seriously. More women are able to define their own identities. More women are in the public sphere. The women's rights movement, in short, has transformed—not died.

Today, women mobilize around new, universal objectives, such as environmental protection, domestic violence, child safety, and human rights. On May 14, 2000, Mother's Day, women organized a Million Mom March in Washington, DC, to call for stricter gun control in response to the spate of violent gun deaths in recent years. Many women's rights groups, including NOW, attended. Representative Carolyn McCarthy of New York told the crowd, "When a mother is trying to protect a child, don't mess with us." And feminists continue to grapple with male-female relations. Should fathers as well as mothers be given leave after the birth of a child? Is pornography oppressive to women, or important to female sexual freedom?

Women at War

Although women had been integrated into the military, the Combat Exclusion Law was still in effect in the 1990s. In the 1991 Gulf War, 35,000 of the 540,000 members of U.S. military troops were women. They were allowed into combat areas for the purpose of transporting fuel, food, and troops. They maintained equipment, operated communication equipment, and developed intelligence information. Two women were taken prisoner and eleven lost their lives.

Later that year, the U.S. Senate voted overwhelmingly to open combat positions to women aviators. By 1995, ten women flew combat aircraft.

Critics of combat exclusion charged that the law was used to restrict the number of women in the military. Yet the issue of whether women should engage in combat remains controversial. A 1992 poll showed that the American public was about equally divided over it. Military officials also continue to wrestle with questions of unisex training and facilities, integration's effect on "readiness, cohesion, and morale," and the issue of sexual harassment.

In 1991, the Tailhook scandal brought sexual harassment in the military to national attention. Lt. Paula Coughlin, an admiral's aide, charged that drunken navy officers fondled and harassed at least five women, including herself and one who was stripped of her clothes, at the Tailhook Association Convention in Las Vegas. The Navy announced it had sent the names of seventy men to their commanding officers for possible disciplinary action. In 1992, Army Specialist Jacqueline Ortiz charged that she had been sexually assaulted by a superior while serving in Saudi Arabia during the Gulf War.

Later that year, the navy took steps to address the problem, ordering a servicewide "stand-down" to give every member of the navy training on sexual harassment. The navy also permanently severed its ties to the Tailhook Association. A Standing Committee on Women in the Navy and the Marine Corps was created to review sexual harassment policies and hear victims' complaints.

There are signs that positive change has taken place. In 1997, a *Washington Post* reporter spent a week with integrated troops in Bosnia and found that male and female military personnel worked together successfully. Few problems arose from the shared living space and lack of privacy. The reporter found that being involved in a purposeful mission limited the incidence of unacceptable behavior.

Abortion: A Continuing Crisis

Although family-planning clinics continue to be targeted by antiabortion groups, the work of pro-choice activists helps to contain the violence. In November 1993, overwhelming majorities in both the House and the Senate passed the Freedom of Access to Clinic Entrances Act (FACE). In May 1994, President Clinton signed the act into law. FACE provides federal criminal and civil penalties for acts of force, the threat of force, and acts of physical obstruction targeted at those providing or seeking to obtain abortion services. By 1998, fewer clinics reported violations of FACE to federal law enforcement officials than ever before. At the same time, federal officials responded more quickly to FACE reports with civil and criminal actions.

Meanwhile, in the 1990s, antiabortion extremists turned to a new tactic: murdering individual doctors who perform abortions. In 1993, Dr. David Gunn was killed outside a clinic in Pensacola, Florida; Dr. George Tiller was shot outside of his clinic in Wichita, Kansas; and Dr. Wayne Patterson was killed in Mobile, Alabama. In 1994, Dr. John Bayard Britton and his escort, James Barrett, were killed in Pensacola. The tactic of shooting doctors spread to neighboring countries. That same year, Dr. Garson Romalis was shot at home in Vancouver, Canada.

In October 1998, a sniper shot Dr. Barnett Slepian in his own home. Within hours of his murder, his name appeared on The Nuremberg Files, an Internet site that lists the addresses and names of family members of abortion doctors. His name had a line through it, indicating that he was a "fatality."

Activists in favor of a woman's right to choose continue to defend that right in the courts. A U.S. Supreme Court ruling gave states the power to place restrictions on women seeking abortions, as long as they are not illegal. These restrictions include imposed waiting periods, gag rules on abortion counseling, and parental consent laws. Meanwhile, antiabortion conservatives started to fill the state legislatures, making it even more difficult to get an abortion. According to the National Abortion and Reproductive Rights Action League (NARAL), in 1999 alone, 439 antiabortion measures were introduced around the country. The main legal objective of antiabortion groups is to get the Supreme Court to reverse its 1973 *Roe v. Wade* decision. Pro-choice activists have increased their efforts to inform the public about voting for politicians who are pro-choice.

RU-486, or Mifepristone

Antiabortion forces have also been effective in limiting other reproductive choices for women. Aside from closing down virtually all federal and private research on contraceptives in the 1980s, they took on RU-486, or Mifepristone. Available in France since 1988, the drug is a safe, nonsurgical way to terminate a pregnancy within the first trimester. Antiabortion groups called RU-486 the "abortion pill" and scrambled to find ways to keep it out of this country, despite its potential to also treat fibroid tumors, ovarian cancer, endometriosis, meningioma, and some types of breast cancer.

Throughout the 1990s, the Feminist Majority Foundation, founded in 1987, took on the challenge of bringing RU-486 to the United States. The Feminist Majority led delegations of scientists and feminist leaders to urge the manufacturers of RU-486 to bring it to the United States, carrying with them 115,000 petitions from American citizens who supported the drug. President Clinton also encouraged its research and development. Through the efforts of pro-choice activists, contraception that can prevent pregnancy up to seventy-two hours after intercourse was approved by the U.S. government and marketed since 1998. The Food and Drug Administration approved of restricted use of RU-486 in September 2000.

Women's Health

In 1991, NOW urged the National Institutes of Health (NIH), a leading body in the field of medical research, to design a long-term research plan to improve the health and lives of American women. Breast cancer, which ranks just behind lung cancer as the leading cause of cancer death for women, attacks one in every eight American women and kills 46,000 women a year. The disease is of particular concern to African American women since African American women are more likely than white women to die from it, although white women are more likely than African American women to get the disease. The reason for this anomaly may be unequal access to preventive care and treatment.

Thanks to the work of feminist groups, more funds have been allocated for breast cancer research.

In 1992, Congress approved a budget of more than $400 million for breast cancer research, three times the amount of the previous year's budget. Congress approved $15.5 billion in NIH funding for 1999, $479 million of which went to breast cancer research. The good news is that death rates from most of the leading killers of women, including heart disease, dropped significantly between 1970 and 1993 for both African American and white women. The exceptions were cancer, chronic obstructive pulmonary disease, and AIDS.

Feminist organizations continue to address issues related to the health of American women. For example, substantial sex bias exists in Medicare and Medicaid reimbursement for female-specific medical procedures. Although women make up 57 percent of Medicare recipients and 58.5 percent of the adult recipients of Medicaid, both Medicare and Medicaid reimburse only 60 percent of obstetrics and gynecology expenses compared with 91 percent of urology practice expenses. Furthermore, in some clinical trials, women are either excluded or under-represented. Thus, the conclusions for diagnosis and treatment drawn from these trials are skewed to the disadvantage of women.

One of the major issues facing feminist activists today is discrimination in the health insurance industry. Women of childbearing age are frequently forced to pay higher premiums on the basis that they may incur the high costs of pregnancy. Many health insurers do not adequately cover illnesses and conditions specific to women. Women of reproductive age spend 68 percent more than men on out-of-pocket health care costs, including contraceptives and reproductive health care. In 1999, nine states passed laws requiring contraceptive coverage in insurance plans.

Sexual Violence

In the 1970s, as a result of the women's rights movement, violence against women came to be viewed as a serious social problem for the first time. A national survey in 1995–1996 found that as many as 1.9 million women are physically assaulted annually. Assault covers a range of behaviors, including being hit, raped, and the victim of weapons. The survey also found most violence against women is perpetrated by their partners and that women experience more violence from partners than do men.

The passage of the Violence Against Women Act (VAWA) in 1994 was the first major attempt to deal with domestic violence and sexual assault. Before this law, which provides tough federal penalties, an abuser could beat his wife and escape prosecution simply by taking her across state borders—crossing the state line created problems of jurisdiction. In 1995, the first case to be prosecuted under VAWA resulted in the conviction of a West Virginia man who, according to court testimony, beat his wife into unconsciousness and locked her in the trunk of her car. He then drove back and forth between West Virginia and Kentucky for six days but never sought medical attention for his wife, who lapsed into a coma.

NOW and the National Task Force on Violence Against Women lobbied for expanded legislation that became known as VAWA II. The Violence Against Women Act of

1998 contained $1 billion for the construction of women's shelters. It proposed initiatives for understanding battering in the workplace, specifically in cases of low-income and welfare-to-work participants, who are shown to be especially vulnerable; for improved health services for survivors; for better law enforcement and prevention; and for better education about battering.

Women's Rights Are Human Rights

The women's rights movement of today encompasses a much wider range of issues. Discrimination that united women in the 1960s and 1970s still affects women on the fringes of society as strongly as it ever did.

Today, lesbians and gays are vocal about the numerous issues affecting them: HIV and other health issues, civil rights, domestic partnership and marriage, hate crimes, and education. They continue to confront discrimination in the workplace, housing, and public venues. According to one study, a lesbian earns up to 14 percent less than a heterosexual woman with a similar background, because of discrimination on the basis of her sexual orientation.

Issues of health and medical access were at the forefront of the gay and lesbian movement in the 1980s, but they are being superseded by concerns about antigay and antilesbian violence. In 1998, hate crime made the headlines when a twenty-one-year-old man, Matthew Shepherd, was brutally murdered. The openly gay student at the University of Wyoming was savagely beaten to death, burned, and

tied to a wooden fence. Such incidents have drawn attention to the need for broader hate-crime laws. One private
organization that tracks gender-based violence reported
that antigay hate crimes are becoming increasingly brutal,
involving the use of weapons such as guns, ropes, and
bats. Feminists join gay and lesbian groups and groups
like the Anti-Defamation League in the pursuit of stronger
laws to help prosecute murders motivated by the gender,
sexual orientation, or disability of the victim. Hate-crime
bills have been introduced in seven states; one introduced
in Kentucky did not include sexual orientation.

Women Around the World

Elsewhere in the world, women face similar issues and
struggle with them to varying degrees of success. In August
1999, *The Times* of London reported that "the ugly and militant tactics of American antiabortionism" closed a family-
planning clinic that had been operating in Northern Ireland
for over twenty years. The clinic referred its cases to the
Family Planning Association in Belfast, which is equipped
to defend itself against antiabortion terrorism.

In Botswana, where many women suffer from domestic
abuse, the first shelter for abused women was formed in
1989. The shelter counsels husbands as well as wives when-
ever possible, since it is thought that the country's traditional values of male superiority and female servitude
encourage violence against women.

In some countries, women face extreme hardship. In
1984, the president of Romania, Nicolae Ceausescu,
declared it the "patriotic duty" of Romanian women to

Leading the Way

In 1988, Benazir Bhutto was sworn in as the first woman to lead an Islamic country, Pakistan. She announced a program to end restrictions on women and promised maternity leave, equal pay for equal work, and a minimum wage. She served two terms as prime minister, in 1988–1990 and in 1993–1996.

bear four children, and he announced "stern measures" against abortion to be enforced by the police. Married women had to undergo monthly pregnancy tests at their workplaces and had to have a medical explanation for "persistent nonpregnancy." Should the police decide that a woman had lied about an abortion, she could face a year in prison. Many women died from illegal abortions. Women who did not conceive could lose their jobs. Although Ceausescu was killed in a revolution in 1989, he has left a legacy that includes the highest abortion rate in Europe and the highest rate of pregnancy mortality.

American feminists often take up the causes of women in other oppressive societies, especially women who have fewer opportunities to improve their conditions. When more than 100 Filipino, Sri Lankan, and other foreign women reported being raped or badly beaten by Kuwaiti soldiers, police, and Kuwaiti citizens in whose homes they worked, the Feminist Majority stepped into action. Feminist Majority president Eleanor Smeal set up an emergency hotline and urged the public to flood the Kuwait Embassy and the United States State Department with protest letters. They urged immediate action in response to the widely reported accounts that hundreds of Asian women workers were being raped or beaten by their Kuwaiti employers and had taken refuge in their countries' embassies. Representative Patricia Schroeder was denied a visa to visit Kuwait to investigate the reports.

The *New York Times* reported that every day fifteen to twenty Filipino, Sri Lankan, and other foreign women brought to Kuwait as domestic servants sought refuge in their countries' embassies. The Philippine Embassy alone sheltered 130 of these refugees. They complained of beatings, sexual abuse, late or nonpayment of salaries, no time off, and being denied contact with the outside world. They were not permitted to leave the country without an exit visa, and the Kuwaiti government would not issue exit visas without their employers' consent. Often, unless they could raise the $1,500 to cover their employers' cost in bringing them to Kuwait, the women were trapped, unable to work and unable to leave.

Under the rule of the Taliban, an Afghani militia group, women have few human rights. They live under virtual "house arrest," banned from going to school, having jobs, or even leaving the house unless escorted by a male relative. They have been beaten, tortured, and killed for violating these laws. In response, the Feminist Majority has

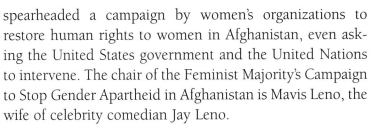

Blazing New Trails

Despite the persistent predominance of men's sports on both the college and professional level, the Women's National Basketball Association (WNBA) emerged on April 24, 1996. A hopeful sign of things to come, the all-male National Basketball Association (NBA) approved the concept of a women's league to begin play in 1997. Supported by female and male fans alike, WNBA games are broadcast on three major television networks.

spearheaded a campaign by women's organizations to restore human rights to women in Afghanistan, even asking the United States government and the United Nations to intervene. The chair of the Feminist Majority's Campaign to Stop Gender Apartheid in Afghanistan is Mavis Leno, the wife of celebrity comedian Jay Leno.

Around the world, women and children are exploited in factories where they work for wages that are below poverty level. American companies own many of these sweatshops. In 1996, NOW passed a resolution to expose such companies and labor practices. One American sports clothing manufacturer, for example, has operated production plants all over Asia. Investigators found that its workers, mostly women, earned less than $1.60 a day. They were also subjected to sexual harassment, verbal abuse, and corporal punishment.

123

Women's rights in the workplace have come a long way in recent decades, but there is still much progress to be made.

On September 11, 1995, 109 countries met in Beijing for the Fourth World Conference on Women. Delegates to the conference discussed ways to change the condition of women in their countries. They made commitments for change in the areas of economic empowerment, women's social advancement, and health. Fewer commitments were made to address media images of women, the environment, and the issue of armed conflict. Among the forty-seven countries that made specific commitments based upon conference recommendations, Australia committed to introduce a new health program for indigenous women; Cambodia promised to ensure gender parity on peace negotiation and conflict resolution bodies; India promised to focus on girls' education; the Ukraine committed to a national family planning program; and the United States agreed to launch a six-year initiative against domestic violence.

A Look Back and Forward

Today, the best way to understand how far women in the United States have come in the last century is to compare the lives of women and girls in the past to how women and girls live today. A century ago, women could not own property, vote, or have careers. It is hard to imagine such times. Fifty years ago, most women had few choices besides raising a family, and if they worked they had few opportunities. Just three decades ago, a married woman could not get a credit card in her own name. Most women could not get a bank loan without a male cosigner, such as a father, brother, or husband. Until 1976, women had to get their husband's consent to get an abortion. Single girls under eighteen had to get permission from a parent.

How much have attitudes changed? Even today, men are encouraged to work, while working women are still made to feel guilty for "abandoning" the family. Twenty years after the passage of Title IX prohibiting sex discrimination in education, a 1992 report issued by the National Collegiate Athletic Association (NCAA) documented the persistence of bias in favor of men. For example, the gap in recruiting expenses was nearly five to one.

One hundred and fifty years after Seneca Falls, women still do not have equal representation. In the United States, women make up only 12 percent of the members of Congress. There were only three female governors as of 1998. No woman has ever served as president, vice president, speaker of the House of Representatives, or majority leader of the Senate, and only rarely as a full committee chair of either body of Congress. Yet the women's movement has brought about many of the things we take for granted. And the progress continues.

• In 1997, Madeleine Albright became the first woman to serve as United States secretary of state, becoming one of the highest-ranking woman government official's in United States history.

• In April 1999, Eileen M. Colleens led a crew of five on space shuttle *Columbia*, as the first female space shuttle commander. The mission objective was to launch the Chandra X-ray Observatory, which collects data on exploding stars, quasars, and black holes.

• In sports, high-profile athletes such as Mia Hamm, whose team led the United States to victory in the 1999 Women's World Cup Soccer Championship, are bringing new excitement to women's sports and serving as role models for new generations of girls.

Women today have the opportunity and the challenge of uniting on common ground in spite of differences in age, race, culture, and economic class. As organizers of the Million Mom March proved, women are a powerful force who can do much to change the world. The facts show that women have come a long way but that it's not yet time for women to let down their guard.

Preamble to the Constitution

We the People of the United States, in order to form a more perfect Union, establish Justice, insure domestic Tranquility, provide for the common defence, promote the general Welfare, and secure the Blessings of Liberty to ourselves and our Posterity, do ordain and establish this Constitution for the United States of America.

On September 25, 1789, Congress transmitted to the state legislatures twelve proposed amendments, two of which, having to do with congressional representation and congressional pay, were not adopted. The remaining ten amendments became the Bill of Rights.

The Bill of Rights

Amendment I

Congress shall make no law respecting an establishment of religion, or prohibiting the free exercise thereof; or abridging the freedom of speech, or of the press; or the right of the people peaceably to assemble, and to petition the Government for a redress of grievances.

Amendment II

A well regulated Militia, being necessary to the security of a free State, the right of the people to keep and bear Arms, shall not be infringed.

Amendment III

No Soldier shall, in time of peace be quartered in any house, without the consent of the Owner, nor in time of war, but in a manner to be prescribed by law.

Amendment IV

The right of the people to be secure in their persons, houses, papers, and effects, against unreasonable searches and seizures, shall not be violated, and no Warrants shall issue, but upon probable cause, supported by Oath or affirmation, and particularly describing the place to be searched, and the persons or things to be seized.

Amendment V

No person shall be held to answer for a capital, or otherwise infamous crime, unless on a presentment or indictment of a Grand Jury, except in cases arising in the land or naval forces, or in the Militia, when in actual service in time of War or public danger; nor shall any person be subject for the same offence to be twice put in jeopardy of life or limb; nor shall be compelled in any criminal case to be a witness against himself, nor be deprived of life, liberty, or property, without due process of law; nor shall private property be taken for public use, without just compensation.

Amendment VI

In all criminal prosecutions, the accused shall enjoy the right to a speedy and public trial, by an impartial jury of the State and district wherein the crime shall have been committed, which district shall have been previously ascertained by law, and to be informed of the nature and cause of the accusation; to be confronted with the witnesses against him; to have compulsory process for obtaining witnesses in his favor, and to have the Assistance of Counsel for his defence.

Amendment VII

In Suits at common law, where the value in controversy shall exceed twenty dollars, the right of trial by jury shall be preserved, and no fact tried by a jury, shall be otherwise re-examined in any Court of the United States, than according to the rules of the common law.

Amendment VIII

Excessive bail shall not be required, nor excessive fines imposed, nor cruel and unusual punishments inflicted.

Amendment IX

The enumeration in the Constitution, of certain rights, shall not be construed to deny or disparage others retained by the people.

Amendment X

The powers not delegated to the United States by the Constitution, nor prohibited by it to the States, are reserved to the States respectively, or to the people.

Glossary

abolitionism   Measures or principles to abolish an institution, such as slavery in the United States.

activism   Practice of making social or political change through direct action, such as mass demonstrations.

affiliation   Association with a group or organization as a member.

agrarian   Relating to the farming or ownership of land.

amendment   Formal alteration, especially of a law, bill, or motion.

antebellum   Existing before a war, especially before the Civil War.

article   Distinct part of a written document, such as a constitution or piece of legislation.

backlash   Strong reaction against some prior development, especially some political or social change.

ballot Piece of paper on which a voter enters his or her vote.

boycott To refuse to buy, use, attend, or deal with (a product, activity, business, or the like), usually as a protest or means of persuasion.

candidate Person who offers himself or herself or is proposed by others as a suitable person for an office or honor.

capitalism Economic system characterized by private ownership rather than government control of capital goods, and by the distribution of goods as determined by competition in a free market.

common law Body of law developed in England based on custom and precedent that makes up the basis of the legal system in the United States, except in Louisiana.

conservative Favoring a policy of keeping things as they are, in opposition to change.

constitution Basic principles and laws of a nation, state, or social group that determine the powers and duties of government and guarantee certain rights to the people in it.

constitutionality Quality of being in agreement with the provisions of a constitution.

contemporaneous Existing during the same time.

convention An assembly of people gathered together for a common purpose.

decentralize To transfer functions or powers from a central authority to regional or local authorities.

discrimination Difference, and especially an unjust

difference, in the way a person or group is treated in comparison with another.

elitist   One who believes in the social superiority of one group over others.

esoteric   Understood or known only by a few persons who have special training or interests.

feminism   The theory of advocating the same social, political, and economic rights for women as for men; the movement dedicated to achieving these rights.

gag rule   Rule or law that restricts discussion of a particular topic, especially in a legislative body.

grassroots   At the local level as opposed to in political or cultural centers.

habeas corpus   A writ issued by a court commanding that a person held in custody be brought before a court so that it may determine whether the detention is lawful

injustice   Violation of a person's rights; an unjust act or deed.

legislation   The laws that are made.

legislature   A body of persons having the power to make, alter, or repeal laws.

liberal   Based upon the ideals of social change.

lobby   To conduct activities aimed at influencing government officials or at securing passage of legislation.

matriarchal   Characterized by rule of a family, group, or state by a woman or women.

militant   Aggressive or hostile in attitude or actions, especially in defense of a cause.

paternalistic   Characterized by rule of individuals

in a paternal manner, by taking care of their needs but giving them virtually no responsibility.

patriarchal   Characterized by rule of a family, group, or state by a man or men.

patriotic   Having or showing patriotism, love of one's country, and devotion to its welfare.

petition   Formal written request addressed to an official person or group.

radical   Departing sharply from the usual or traditional; a person who favors rapid and sweeping changes in laws or methods of government.

ratification   The act of approving or sanctioning formally.

referendum   The practice of submitting a measure to popular vote.

reform   The removal or correction of an abuse, a wrong, or an error.

repeal   To do away with, especially by legislative action.

republic   A government in which ultimate power resides in the citizens entitled to vote.

rhetoric   The art of using language effectively in speech or writing, especially to influence or persuade one's audience.

sovereign   Supreme in power or authority.

statute   A law enacted by a legislative body.

suffragette   An advocate of women's right to vote.

union   Group of workers organized to advance or protect their rights and interests.

writ   An order in writing signed by an officer of the court or judicial officer.

For More Information

Feminist Majority Organization
1600 Wilson Boulevard, Suite 801
Arlington, VA 22209
(703) 522-2214
e-mail: femmaj@feminist.org
Web site: http://www.feminist.org/

Girls Incorporated National Resource Center
441 West Michigan Street
Indianapolis, IN 46202-3233
(317) 634-7546
e-mail: girlsinc@girls-inc.org
Web site: http://www.girlsinc.com/

Institute for Women's Policy Research
1707 L Street NW, Suite 750
Washington, DC 20036
(202) 785-5100
e-mail: iwpr@iwpr.org
Web site: http://www.iwpr.org/

League of Women Voters
1730 M Street NW, Suite 1000
Washington, DC 20036-4508
(202) 429-1965
Web site: http://www.lwv.org/

National Organization for Women (NOW)
733 15th Street NW, 2nd floor
Washington, DC 20005
(202) 628-8NOW (8669)
e-mail: now@now.org
Web site: http://www.now.org/

National Women's Hall of Fame
76 Fall Street
P.O. Box 335
Seneca Falls, NY 13148
(315) 568-8060
e-mail: greatwomen@greatwomen.org
Web site: http://www.greatwomen.org/

National Women's History Project
7738 Bell Road
Windsor, CA 95492
(707) 838-6000
e-mail: nwhp@aol.com
Web site: http://www.nwhp.org/

United Nations WomenWatch
e-mail: womenwatch@un.org
Web site: http://www.un.org/womenwatch/

Women's College Coalition
125 Michigan Avenue NE
Washington, DC 20017
(202) 234-0443
e-mail: msm@trinitydc.edu
Web site: http://www.academic.org

Women's Leadership Fund
Web site: http://www.womensleadershipfund.org/

YWCA of the U.S.A.
Empire State Building
350 Fifth Avenue, Suite 301
New York, NY 10118
(212) 273-7800
Web site: http://www.ywca.org/

For Further Reading

Berkin, Carol Ruth, and Mary Beth Norton. *Women of America: A History*. Boston: Houghton Mifflin Company, 1979.

Clinton, Catherine. *The Other Civil War: American Women in the Nineteenth Century*. New York: Farrar, Straus & Giroux, 1999.

Drill, Esther, Heather McDonald, and Rebecca Odes. *Deal with It! A New Approach to Your Body, Brain, and Life as a Gurl*. New York: Pocket Books, 1999.

Faludi, Susan. *Backlash: The Undeclared War Against American Women*. New York: Anchor Books, 1992.

Fox-Genovese, Elizabeth. *Feminism Is Not the Story of My Life*. New York: Anchor Books, 1997.

Friedan, Betty. *The Feminine Mystique*. New York: Dell Publishing Co., 1984.

Giddings, Paula. *When and Where I Enter: The Impact of Black Women on Race and Sex in America*. New York: Morrow, 1984.

Lloyd, Trevor Owen. *Suffragettes International: The World-*

Wide Campaign for Women's Rights. New York: American Heritage Press, 1971.

Lunardini, Christine. *What Every American Should Know About Women's History*. Holbrook, MA: Adams Media Corporation, 1996.

Ms. Foundation for Women. *Girls Seen and Heard: 52 Life Lessons for Our Daughters*. New York: Putnam Publishing Group, 1998.

Rossi, Alice S., ed. *The Feminist Papers: From Adams to De Beauvoir*. Boston: Northeastern University Press, 1988.

Index

League of Self–Supporting
    Women, 48, 52
League of Women Voters, 64, 68,
    72, 84, 86, 90
Lowell Female Labor Reform
    Association, 27
Lucretia Mott Amendment, 65

M

McCarthy, Carolyn, 111
McShane, Elizabeth, 55–56
militancy, 27–28, 52, 53–56, 57,
    85
military, women in, 70–71,
    93–95, 105–106
Million Mom March, 111, 127
Minor v. Happersett, 42
Mott, Lucretia, 28, 29
Mount Holyoke College, 26
Ms. magazine, 87–89
Murray, Judith Sargent
    Stevens, 25

N

National Abortion and
    Reproductive Rights Action
    League (NARAL), 114
National American Women's
    Suffrage Association
    (NAWSA), 33, 44–45, 46,
    47, 48, 54, 56, 57–58, 59,
    63–64, 65
National Association for the
    Advancement of Colored
    People (NAACP), 72, 73
National Association of Colored
    Women (NACW), 32, 33,
    68–69, 92
National Association of Wage
    Earners, 66

National Black Feminist
    Organization, 92–93
National Council of Negro
    Women (NCNW), 69, 92
National Federation of
    Afro–American Women, 32
National League of Colored
    Women, 32
National Organization for
    Women (NOW), 83–85, 86,
    95, 100, 102–103, 111,
    115, 118, 123
National Welfare Rights
    Organization, 92
National Woman's Party (NWP),
    54, 55, 56, 65, 66, 72, 79
National Women's Political
    Caucus, 93
National Women's Suffrage
    Association (NWSA), 39,
    40, 41, 42, 44
Nineteenth Amendment, 15, 59, 63
    ratification of, 60

O

Oberlin College, 26, 32

P

Pankhurst, Emmeline, 27–28,
    52, 54
Parks, Rosa, 72
Paul, Alice, 53–55, 57
Peterson, Esther, 78
Philadelphia Female Anti–Slavery
    Society, 28, 32
postfeminism, 98
President's Commission on the
    Status of Women, 77–78, 79
Progressive Era, 49–50
Purvis, Harriet Forten, 31–32, 36
Purvis, Hattie, 36

141

Acknowledgements
Jacqueline would like to thank her past and present editors at Rosen for the continuing fellowship and productive cooperation.

Photo Credits
Cover image: The Constitution of the United States of America; p. 12 © Joseph Sohm/ChromoSohm Inc./Corbis; p. 29 © Bettmann/Corbis; p. 33 © Corbis; p. 38 © Bettmann/Corbis; p. 51 © Illustration from the Jim Zwick Collection; p. 59 © Corbis; p. 65 © Archive Photos; p. 67 © Bettmann/Corbis; p. 73 © Bettmann/Corbis; p. 85 © Richard Watson/Archive Photos; p. 88 © Ms.Magazine Corp.; p. 94 © UPI/Bettmann/Corbis; p. 101 © Owen Franken/Corbis; p. 105 © Leif Skoogfors/Corbis; p. 107 © Corbis; p. 116 © Royalty Free/Corbis; p. 121 © Francoise de Mulder/Corbis; p. 123 © Corbis; p. 124 © Ken Reid/FPG.

Series Design and Layout
Danielle Goldblatt